Aleene's CHRISTMAS Craft Quickies

Designs by Heidi Borchers

Oxmoor House

Aleene's
CHRISTMAS
Craft Quickies

Aleene's® Christmas Craft Quickies
from the *Best of ALEENE'S CREATIVE LIVING®* series
©1996 by Oxmoor House, Inc.
Book Division of Southern Progress Corporation
P.O. Box 2463, Birmingham, Alabama 35201

Published by Oxmoor House, Inc., and Leisure Arts, Inc.

Library of Congress Card Catalog Number: 96-68031
Hardcover ISBN: 0-8487-1510-1
Softcover ISBN: 0-8487-1511-X
Manufactured in the United States of America
First Printing 1996

Aleene's® is a registered trademark of Artis, Inc.
Trademark Registration #1504878
Aleene's® is used by permission of Artis, Inc.

Designs by Heidi Borchers

Editor-in-Chief: Nancy Fitzpatrick Wyatt
Senior Crafts Editor: Susan Ramey Cleveland
Senior Editor, Editorial Services: Olivia Kindig Wells
Art Director: James Boone

Aleene's® Christmas Craft Quickies

Editor: Margaret Allen Price
Editorial Assistant: Barzella Estle
Copy Editor: L. Amanda Owens
Senior Photographer: John O'Hagan
Photographer: Jeff Lapidis
Photo Stylist: Connie Formby
Assistant Art Director: Cynthia R. Cooper
Designer: Carol Damksy
Illustrator: Kelly Davis
Senior Production Designer: Larry Hunter
Publishing Systems Administrator: Rick Tucker
Production and Distribution Director: Phillip Lee
Associate Production Manager: Theresa L. Beste
Production Coordinator: Marianne Jordan Wilson
Production Assistant: Valerie Heard

CONTENTS

Aleene's Christmas Album

Seasonal Trims
Create handmade decorations
to use in your holiday home.

Page 34

Crafty Holiday Gifts
58

Showcase your crafting talents with one or more of these great gifts.

Page 74

Page 76

Tips for Better Crafting
136

Learn the secrets to Heidi's crafting success.

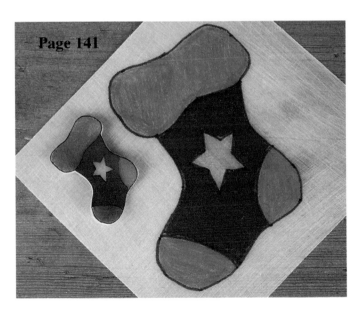

Page 141

Festive Fashions
102

Craft a wardrobe full of seasonal style with this selection of easy designs.

Page 114

Index
144

Heidi made most of the decorations for my tree. Turn to page 13 for more information on the ornaments.

When Christmas is on a weekday, our television show is on the air as usual. One year, Heidi, Tiffany, and I wore flannel nightgowns for the opening and closing segments of the Christmas Day show.

Aleene's Christmas Album

On the day after Thanksgiving, Heidi and I begin putting up my Christmas decorations. We start at the front door and add a touch of holiday cheer to every room in my home. As you'll see in the following pages, many of the decorations are handcrafted items that you can make for your home. In addition, there is a chapter devoted to gifts and another chapter full of seasonal wearables. So get ready to display your creativity and share your talents with others through your very own handmade Christmas.

I have always involved my family in preparing for the holidays. Everyone pitches in to help get the house ready. Even the grandchildren and great-grandchildren help make some of the decorations. It helps us get in the spirit of the season when we spend time together crafting and decorating. Anticipation of the coming holiday and the joy of expressing our creativity is as much fun as the big day itself. If you get everyone involved and set the goal of doing a little bit of decorating every day, you can trim your entire house in plenty of time to enjoy the holidays.

Heidi makes the invitations for the family party. Each party has a theme, and everyone gets a chance to participate in a creative way.

My grandchildren and great-grandchildren help make the holiday magical.

The Family Party

Heidi is in charge of planning the family Christmas party. Each year she picks a theme or a game for us to play, and she makes all the invitations. This year each family put together a themed gift basket and brought it wrapped up in a garbage bag. Tiffany unwrapped the baskets and arranged them on a table. We each tried to guess who had created each basket. The person who matched the most baskets with the correct creators got to choose a basket to take home. Then the person who created the chosen basket picked his or her choice of basket from the remaining ones and so on.

Our family is so large that it is almost impossible to buy a gift for each member. By setting a dollar limit on the basket and asking each household to bring only one, we make the party more affordable for everyone. This party is a fun way for us to laugh and to spend time together.

Christmas can be a very hectic time, so be sure to spend a moment laughing and crafting with someone special this holiday season. You'll find the true meaning of the holidays in those shared moments.

Wishing you the happiest of holidays,

Aleene

My family gathers for the annual Christmas portrait.

The baskets were arranged on the table, and each person tried to guess who had brought which basket.

Seasonal Trims

Start decorating at your front door and don't stop until every room in the house has a touch of holiday color. In these pages, you'll see the decorations Heidi created for Aleene's house, plus lots of designs to dress up your home for the holidays.

Country Angels Tree

Aleene's Family Trees

Both of the trees shown here feature Aleene's favorite theme: angels. Choose a theme for your tree and use a mixture of handmade and purchased decorations in keeping with your theme.

Country Angels Tree

When Heidi and Aleene prepare to decorate for Christmas, first they decide on a theme. "My tree is always decorated with a mixture of handmade ornaments and store-bought treasures," says Aleene. "For this tree, Heidi made faux stained-glass angels, red-and-gold balls, and icicles." (Directions for ornaments are on pages 16 and 17.) Heidi complemented these handmade ornaments with twisted-bead garlands, metallic corkscrew garland, purchased balls in a variety of colors, and a few silk tassels. Raffia bows and baby's breath add an airy look to the tree.

To make the twisted-bead garland, Heidi wound three strands together: pearls, red beads, and gold beads. She used florist's wire to secure the ends. For the corkscrew garland, she wrapped wired cording and gold metallic wire around a large marking pen to coil them.

A Gold-and-White Tree

This angel tree is more formal than the Country Angels Tree. White wire angels, clear plastic snowflakes and icicles, and gold metallic bows establish the dressier color scheme here. A large multilooped bow serves as a tree topper. "I like to hang angels from the ceiling near the top of my tree," says Aleene. "The lengths of ribbon and pearl string draped from the tree to the ceiling link the angels to the tree." Drifts of purchased snow on the branches add the finishing touch to the decorations.

A Gold-and-White Tree

Tree-Trimming Tips

Once you've selected the perfect tree, it's time to trim it. Learn the secrets to tree trimming by following the five easy steps outlined here.

1 To **arrange the lights,** begin at the top of the tree and work down. Instead of garlanding the tree with lights, place lights along each branch. Beginning near the trunk, bring the lights out to the branch tip and then back to the trunk. Use lots of lights.

2 To **fill in gaps** where the tree doesn't have branches or to hide the light cords, use shredded paper, moss, or 6"-wide lengths of netting or fabric. If you have a very full tree, you may not need to drape the trunk. Even so, if you use fabric in the same color scheme as the ornaments, the drape will emphasize the depth of the tree and soften the look of the trunk.

3 To **garland the tree,** begin at the top and work down and around the tree, draping the garland from branch to branch. Vary the swag lengths. Garland possibilities include paper dolls, paper chains, raffia, popcorn, cranberries, lace, bead strings, and braided silken cord.

4 To **hang the ornaments,** place smaller items higher on the tree and larger items on the lower branches. Icicles add magic and Shrink-It icicles are a quick-and-easy, inexpensive alternative to purchased aluminum ones (see page 17 for directions). Also consider colorful tassels and plastic or glass prisms. Use bows to fill in gaps in the decorations and to unify the look of the tree.

5 For a **finishing touch,** add baby's breath or purchased snow to the tree. Crown the tree with a topper and cover the base of the tree with a skirt in keeping with the theme. Be sure to coordinate the colors of your wrapped packages with the decorations.

Paper Plate Ornaments

Cut pieces from the fluted edge of inexpensive paper plates to make these simple ornaments.

Materials
Patterns on page 46
White posterboard scraps
Heavyweight gold metallic paper
Hole punches: ¼"-diameter, star-shaped
White fluted-edge paper plates
Aleene's Tacky Glue™
Acrylic paints: peach, black, light yellow
Paintbrush
4 (9") lengths gold metallic thread

Directions

1 Transfer patterns and cut the following: 1 wings and 1 triangle from posterboard; 1 halo, 1 heart, 1 large star, and 1 tree trunk from gold metallic paper. Also cut 1 (3¼"-diameter) circle from posterboard for wreath. Center and draw a 1¾"-diameter circle inside 3¼" circle. Cut out center and set aside for angel's head. From gold metallic scraps, punch 11 circles for wreath and 8 stars for tree. From fluted edge of paper plates, cut ½"- to ¾"-long rounded pieces to cover wings, triangle, and wreath (see photo). Also cut 11 (½"-long) comma shapes for angel's hair.

2 **For angel,** beginning at center of wings and overlapping pieces, glue rounded pieces to posterboard to cover angel's wings. Let dry. Paint angel's head peach. Let dry. Dot black on head for eyes. Let dry. Paint hair pieces light yellow. Let dry. Glue hair pieces to head. Glue halo to hair. Let dry. Glue heart and head in place on wings. Let dry.

For wreath, overlap and glue rounded pieces to posterboard to cover wreath. Let dry. Place each gold circle right side down in palm of hand and press with a pencil eraser to shape. Glue gold circles to wreath as desired. Let dry. Tie 1 length of thread in a bow and glue to wreath front. Let dry.

For tree, beginning at bottom of triangle and overlapping pieces, glue rounded pieces to posterboard to cover triangle. Let dry. Glue large star to top of tree. Glue small stars to tree as desired. Glue trunk to back of tree at bottom. Let dry.

3 **For each,** to attach hanger, fold 1 length of gold thread in half to form loop and knot ends. Glue knot to top back of ornament. Let dry.

Stained-Glass Angel Ornament

Heidi made a host of these colorful angels to decorate Aleene's tree. The ornaments are so easy to put together that the whole family can help make them.

Materials (for 1 angel)

Pattern on page 46
Aleene's Clear Shrink-It™ Plastic
Aleene's 3-D Foiling™ Glue
Gold press-and-peel craft foil
Rubber pencil grip (optional)
1-ply sheer paper napkins or tissue paper: green or red, pink, gold
Fabric to protect work surface
½" shader or sponge paintbrush
Aleene's Reverse Collage™ Glue
⅛"-diameter hole punch
6" length gold metallic thread

Directions

Note: Be sure to test paper napkins or tissue paper for colorfastness as glue causes some colors to bleed.

1 Lay Shrink-It on top of pattern. Using 3-D Foiling Glue, trace pattern onto Shrink-It. Let glue dry for about 24 hours. (Glue will be opaque and sticky when dry. Glue must be thoroughly dry before foil is applied.)

2 To apply gold foil, lay foil dull side down on top of glue lines. Using fingers or pencil grip, gently but firmly press foil onto glue, completely covering glue with foil. Be sure to press foil into crevices. Peel away foil paper. If any part of glue lines is not covered, reapply foil as needed.

3 Transfer patterns to paper napkins and cut 1 dress from green or red, 1 face from pink, and 2 wings from gold, adding ¼" all around to each piece. Crumple each napkin piece and then flatten it, leaving some wrinkles. Cover work surface with fabric to protect foiling. Lay Shrink-It, foil side down, on fabric. Working over 1 design area at a time, brush coat of Reverse Collage Glue on Shrink-It in desired position. Press napkin piece into glue-covered area. Working from outside edges to center, use fingers or brush to gently wrinkle napkin, shaping it to fit design area. Brush coat of Reverse Collage Glue on top of napkin. In same manner, glue remaining napkin pieces in place on Shrink-It. Let dry.

4 Cut out angel, cutting close to foil lines. Center and punch hole inside halo for hanger. To attach hanger, fold gold thread in half to form loop and knot ends. Thread folded end of loop through hole in angel. Thread knotted ends through fold and pull tight to secure.

Icicle & Ball Ornaments

Make icicles for your tree from strips of Shrink-It. The glitzy red-and-gold ornaments are foam balls covered with paper napkin pieces and gold foil.

Icicle

Materials (for 1 icicle)
Aleene's Opake Shrink-It™ Plastic
¼"-diameter hole punch
Aleene's Baking Board or nonstick cookie sheet, sprinkled with baby powder
8" length silver metallic thread

Directions

1 Cut 1 (½" x 10¾") strip of Shrink-It, rounding 1 end and cutting other end to form a point. Punch hole in rounded end of strip. Place strip on baking board and bake in oven as described on page 141. While strip is still warm, wrap it around a pencil to twist. Let cool.

2 To attach hanger, fold silver thread in half to form loop and knot ends. Thread folded end of loop through hole in icicle. Thread knotted ends through fold and pull tight to secure.

Ball Ornament

Materials (for 1 ball)
2" length chenille stem
Aleene's Tacky Glue™
3½"-diameter Styrofoam ball
Red paper napkins
Aleene's Paper Napkin Appliqué™ Glue
Sponge paintbrush
Aleene's 3-D Foiling™ Glue
Gold press-and-peel foil
Aleene's Matte Right-On™ Finish (optional)
10" length ¼"-wide gold metallic braid

Directions

1 Bend chenille stem in half to form hanger. Dip stem ends into Tacky Glue and press into foam ball. Let dry.

2 Cut or tear paper napkins into 1" squares. Remove bottom plies to leave napkin squares 1-ply thick. Working over small area at a time, brush coat of Napkin Appliqué Glue on ball. Press paper square into glue-covered area. Brush coat of glue over paper. In same manner, apply additional paper pieces, overlapping them slightly, until entire ball is covered. Let dry.

3 Brush light, uneven coat of 3-D Foiling Glue on entire surface of ball. Let dry for about 24 hours. (Glue will be opaque and sticky when dry. Glue must be thoroughly dry before foil is applied.) To apply gold foil, lay foil dull side down on top of glue-covered area. Using finger, gently but firmly press foil onto glue, completely covering glue with foil. Peel away foil paper. If any part of glue is not covered, reapply foil as needed.

4 If desired, apply 1 coat of finish to ball. Let dry. Thread braid through chenille stem hanger and tie in bow.

Golf Tee Ornaments

Glue a wooden bead to a golf tee to make the basic body for these tiny ornaments. Add assorted trims for the angel, the snowman, and the Santa shown here or use your imagination to create other holiday figures.

Materials

For each: 1 (⅝"-diameter) wooden bead
Paintbrushes: flat, fine-tip
1 white golf tee
Aleene's Designer Tacky Glue™
Toothpicks
For angel: Acrylic paints: peach, pink, black
10" length silver metallic thread
White curly hair
Ribbon: 8" length ⅛"-wide white satin, 11" length
  ½"-wide gold mesh wired-edge
For snowman: Acrylic paints: white, black
Orange dimensional paint
Black paper scrap
2 (¼"-diameter) red pom-poms
1 (¼" x 3") strip print fabric
3" length ⅛"-wide white satin ribbon
For Santa: Patterns on page 46
Acrylic paints: peach, red, black, pink
Felt scraps: red, white
10" length silver metallic thread

Directions

1 **For angel,** paint bead peach. Let dry. With 1 hole at top, glue bead head to golf tee. Let dry. Dip end of paintbrush into pink paint and dot on bead for cheeks. Dip toothpick into black paint and dot on face for eyes. Draw mouth on face with black paint, using fine-tip brush. Let dry.

For snowman, paint bead white. Let dry. With 1 hole at top, glue bead head to golf tee. Let dry. Dip toothpick into black paint and dot on face for eyes and mouth and on golf tee for buttons. Let dry. Dot orange dimensional paint on face for nose. Let dry.

For Santa, paint bead peach and golf tee red. Let dry. With 1 hole at top, glue bead head to golf

tee. Let dry. Using fine-tip brush, paint belt on tee with black. Let dry. Dip end of paintbrush into red paint and dot on face for nose. Dip toothpick into pink paint and dot on face for cheeks. Dip toothpick into black paint and dot on face for eyes. Let dry.

2 **For angel,** to attach hanger, fold silver thread in half to form loop and knot ends. Put glue in hole at top of head. Using toothpick, poke knot of hanger into glue in hole. Let dry. Glue curly hair to top of head. Let dry. Cut white ribbon in half. Tie 1 white ribbon length in bow and glue to neck. Knot center of remaining white ribbon for hands. Glue 1 end at each side of neck for arms. Let dry. Tie gold ribbon in bow and glue to back of angel for wings. Let dry.

For snowman, cut 1 (⅞"-diameter) circle for hat brim and 1 (⅝" x 2¼") strip for hat crown from black paper. Center and cut 1 (¼"-diameter) hole in black circle. Roll hat crown to form a tube. Overlap ends and glue. Let dry. Center and glue crown on brim. Let dry. Glue hat to head. Glue red pom-poms to head for ear muffs. Wrap fabric strip around neck and glue. Let dry. Put glue in hole at top of head inside hat. Fold ribbon in half to form loop. Using toothpick, poke ribbon ends into glue in hole. Let dry.

For Santa, transfer patterns to felt and cut 1 hat from red and 1 mustache and 1 beard from white. From remaining white, cut 1 (¼" x 3") strip for hat trim. Glue beard and mustache to face. To attach hanger, fold silver thread in half to form loop and knot ends. Curve hat into a cone shape, overlapping straight edges and catching knot of hanger in hat tip, and glue. Glue white felt strip around bottom of hat for trim. Let dry. Glue hat to head. Let dry.

This elegant mantel arrangement looks very expensive, but since you probably have most of the materials at your house, you can re-create it very inexpensively. Make angels that will face each other when hanging on the wall and then link them with a pretty piece of tasseled cording. Artificial garland, spray-painted leaves, gold ball ornaments, and baby's breath complete the scene shown here.

Angels on High

Heidi stiffened textured fabric pieces and sprinkled glitter on them to make the angels hanging above Aleene's mantel. She painted large leaves gathered from the yard gold for the wings.

Materials (for 1 angel)

Patterns on page 47
Corrugated cardboard: 11" x 14" piece, 4" x 6" piece
Waxed paper
Textured fabric: 15" x 18" piece, 6" x 7" piece
Aleene's Fabric Stiffener™
3" square cardboard squeegee
Aleene's Designer Tacky Glue™
Gold spray paint
Gold glitter
2 large leaves
3"-diameter white satin ball ornament with chenille stem hanger loop
White curly hair
12" length gold star garland
12" length ½"-wide gold ribbon

Directions

1 Transfer complete body pattern to 11" x 14" cardboard piece and cut out. Transfer arm pattern to remaining cardboard and cut out. Cover work surface with waxed paper.

2 Lay 15" x 18" fabric piece wrong side up on waxed paper. Use cardboard squeegee to apply coat of stiffener to fabric. Be sure stiffener penetrates fabric but does not saturate it. Turn fabric over and squeegee right side with stiffener. Lay fabric right side up on cardboard body. Turn ½" along long side edges of fabric to back of cardboard. Pin fabric in place until stiffener is dry. Referring to photo, gather 1 short end of fabric to fit neck; arrange gathers in skirt as desired. Pin gathers in place until stiffener is dry. In same manner, stiffen remaining fabric and arrange on remaining cardboard to shape arm. Let arm dry for a few hours. Remove cardboard arm from fabric arm. Glue fabric arm in place on angel body. Pin arm in place until dry.

3 Spray-paint right side of angel gold. Sprinkle glitter onto wet paint. Let dry. Shake off excess glitter. Spray-paint both sides of each leaf gold. Let dry. Glue leaves to back of angel for wings (see photo). Let dry. Glue hanger loop on ball in place at neck of angel. Let dry. Glue curly hair to head. Curve star garland into circle for halo and glue to head. Let dry. Tie ribbon in bow and glue to neck. Let dry.

Burnt Brown Bag Reindeer

Burn a layer of glue on brown bag shapes to make these reindeer. The reindeer with its head up is about 10" high.

Materials (for 1 reindeer)
Patterns on page 48
Tracing paper
Brown grocery bags
3" square cardboard squeegee
Aleene's Tacky Glue™
Christmas star garland wire
Black acrylic paint
Paintbrush
Gold paste paint
Clothespins

Directions

1 To make patterns, transfer body pattern to tracing paper for left side of body. Flip paper with traced design and align traced fold line with fold line on pattern. Transfer pattern to tracing paper again for right side of body. Cut out pattern. Repeat to make pattern for head.

2 Cut 2 (14") squares brown bag. Using cardboard squeegee, apply 1 coat of glue to 1 side of 1 bag piece. With edges aligned, press remaining bag piece into glue. Transfer patterns to layered bag and cut 1 body and 1 head. Bend each piece along fold line and shape as desired (see photo). Let dry.

3 For antlers, cut 2 (1¾") lengths, 2 (3½") lengths, and 2 (3") lengths from star garland. Remove stars from garland. To form each antler, wrap 1 (1¾") wire length around 1 (3½") length about ½" from 1 end of longer wire (see photo). In same manner, wrap 1 (3") length ¾" below first wire.

4 Refer to Burnt Brown Bag How-to on page 140 to burn outside surface of each reindeer piece. Let dry. Paint unburned side of each reindeer piece and each antler black. Let dry. To add gold highlights, rub finger in gold paste paint, wipe off excess on paper towel, and gently rub finger over each reindeer piece. Continue adding gold to burned and unburned sides of each until you get desired effect. Repeat to add gold highlights to antlers. Let dry.

5 To assemble reindeer, glue free end of each antler inside head at top (see photo). Use clothespins to hold antlers in place until glue is dry. Referring to photo for desired positioning, glue ¼" at base of head inside body. Glue tip of nose together. Use clothespins to hold pieces together until glue is dry.

Heidi created this nature scene for Aleene's coffee table. To make this arrangement, you'll need a piece of batting, real or artificial greenery, fresh or dried baby's breath, a pair of burnt brown bag reindeer, several votive candles, and a small evergreen tree decorated with a raffia bow.

Glittering Glue Snowflakes

Use glitter glue sticks and your hot-glue gun to create sparkling snowflake ornaments. The glue sticks come in a variety of colors, so you can make them to match your decorating color scheme.

Materials (for 1 snowflake)

Patterns on page 49
Hot-glue release paper (available in crafts stores)
Opalescent hot-glue sticks
Hot-glue gun
10" length silver metallic thread (optional)
White paper (optional)

Directions

1 Lay release paper on top of desired pattern. Apply glue to paper within pattern lines. Let cool. Peel snowflake from release paper. To add optional hanger, fold silver thread in half to form loop and knot ends. Glue knot to back of snowflake. Let dry.

2 To create original snowflakes, draw circle on white paper for desired finished size of snowflake. Lay release paper on top of marked circle. Draw snowflake on release paper with glue as desired, using circle as guide. Be sure to connect all parts of design from center out so that snowflake will hold together when dry.

Alternate method for making snowflakes

If you prefer not to use a hot-glue gun, you can make snowflakes using 1 sheet of Aleene's Opake Shrink-It™ Plastic, Aleene's Tacky Glue™, and iridescent glitter. Lay Shrink-It over pattern. Referring to Tape Tip Diagram on page 130, make tape tip for glue bottle. Apply glue to Shrink-It within pattern lines. Sprinkle generous amount of glitter onto wet glue. Let dry completely (drying can take as long as 2 days). Peel snowflake from Shrink-It. (*Note:* These snowflakes will not be as opaque as those made with opalescent hot glue.) If desired, add hanger to snowflake.

To frame a doorway, deck a garland of artificial greenery with lights, pearl strings, and glittering snowflakes. Add tiny sprigs of baby's breath or colorful small flowers to the garland. Look for artificial garland in discount and crafts stores. For the best effect, buy a garland with branches instead of a boa-type garland.

A Forest of Christmas Trees

Craft a centerpiece of faux stained-glass trees. Use candles in the arrangement to make the trees glow.

Materials (for 1 tree)
Patterns on page 50
2 sheets Aleene's Clear Shrink-It™ Plastic
Tracing paper
Aleene's 3-D Foiling™ Glue
Gold press-and-peel craft foil
Rubber pencil grip (optional)
Fabric to cover work surface
1-ply sheer paper napkins: green, yellow, assorted color scraps
½" shader or sponge paintbrush
Aleene's Reverse Collage™ Glue
Aleene's Tacky Glue™
2" piece 2 x 4 wood
Band saw
Fine-grade sandpaper
Wood stain
Clear acrylic sealer

Directions
Note: Be sure to test paper napkins for colorfastness as glue causes some colors to bleed.

1 For large tree in center of arrangement, transfer largest triangle to Shrink-It. Transfer star to Shrink-It, omitting placement lines. Cut out triangle and star, adding ¼"-wide and ½"-long tab to bottom of star. To make pattern for any of other trees, trace desired triangle onto tracing paper. Align placement lines at bottom of star pattern with top of traced tree and transfer star to tracing paper. Transfer complete pattern to Shrink-It and cut out.

2 For each tree, use 3-D Foiling Glue to outline star and tree, leaving at least ½" free at base of triangle to insert into wooden base. For large tree, draw circles on tree for ornaments, using 3-D Foiling Glue (see photo). For other trees, dot on 3-D Foiling Glue for ornaments (see photo). Let glue dry for about 24 hours. (Glue will be opaque and sticky when dry. Glue must be thoroughly dry before foil is applied.)

3 To apply gold foil, lay foil dull side down on top of glue lines. Using fingers or pencil grip, gently but firmly press foil onto glue, completely covering glue with foil. Be sure to press foil into crevices. Peel away foil paper. If any part of glue lines is not covered, reapply foil as needed.

4 Cover work surface with fabric to protect foiling. Lay tree, foil side down, on fabric. For

large tree, transfer tree pattern to green paper napkin and cut out, adding ¼" all around. Referring to foil lines on tree, cut out circles where ornaments will be positioned. Crumple napkin tree and then flatten it, leaving some wrinkles. Brush coat of Reverse Collage Glue on wrong side of Shrink-It tree. Press napkin tree into glue-covered area. Working from outside edges to center, use fingers or brush to gently wrinkle napkin, shaping it to fit. Brush coat of Reverse Collage Glue on top of napkin. Let dry.

5 Transfer star pattern to yellow paper napkin and cut out, adding ¼" all around. For large tree, from assorted colors of paper napkins, cut circles for ornaments, slightly larger than circles on tree. In same manner as for tree, glue napkin star to Shrink-It star and napkin ornaments in place on tree. Let dry. Glue tab on star to back of large tree at top, using Tacky Glue. Let dry. In same manner, apply green napkin to other trees, omitting circles for ornaments, and yellow napkin to other stars. For each tree, cut second tree of equal size from Shrink-It for stability.

6 Using band saw, cut 2 x 4 as needed to fit bottom of tree. Using band saw, cut ½"-deep slit in base for bottom of tree. Sand base smooth. Apply 2 coats of wood stain, letting dry between coats. Apply 2 coats of sealer, letting dry between coats. Trim side edges at bottom of stained-glass tree and matching Shrink-It tree as needed to fit base. With edges aligned, place Shrink-It tree behind stained glass tree and press both trees into base.

Combine your forest of stained-glass trees with votive candles, greenery, baby's breath, and red ribbon for a table decoration fit for the finest occasions. Using the patterns on page 50, you can make as many trees in assorted sizes as you need for your table.

Holiday Setting

Heidi finished the edges of the felt place mat with real blanket stitching. She used red dimensional paint to simulate blanket stitching around the tiny trees.

Materials

For each: Patterns on page 51
Fabric scraps: green, Christmas print, red
Dimensional paints: red, gold glitter
For napkin ring: Batting scrap
Lightweight cardboard scrap
Aleene's Tacky Glue™
Paper scrap
1"-wide piece toilet tissue tube
Raffia scrap
For mat and napkin: Purchased green fabric
  napkin
Aleene's Fusible Web™
12" x 18" piece red felt
Green embroidery floss and needle

Directions for napkin ring

1 Transfer tree pattern to green fabric and batting and cut 1 each, cutting just inside pattern line. Transfer tree pattern to cardboard. Center and draw 1 (½") square at bottom of tree for trunk. Cut out tree and trunk as 1 piece. Using cardboard tree as guide, cut 1 tree from Christmas print, adding ½" all around. Cut 1 (2¾" x 5¾") strip from red fabric. Cut 1 (½") square from green fabric for trunk.

2 Center and glue batting tree to 1 side of cardboard tree. With batting side down, center cardboard tree on wrong side of Christmas print tree. Squeeze line of glue around edge of cardboard tree. Fold excess fabric to cardboard and press into glue. Glue green fabric tree to back of tree. Let dry. Draw blanket stitches around edge of tree with red dimensional paint (see photo). Referring to pattern, draw star on paper scrap with gold glitter dimensional paint. Let dry. Trim paper even with painted star. Glue star to top of tree. Let dry.

3 Spread glue on outside of toilet tissue ring. Cover ring with red fabric strip, overlapping ends. Spread glue on inside of ring. Fold excess fabric to inside of ring, overlapping edges. Let dry. Glue green fabric trunk to 1 side of napkin ring (see photo). Let dry. Cut ¾"-long slit in ring above trunk to hold tree. Outline trunk with red dimensional paint. Let dry. Tie raffia in bow and glue to trunk below slit. Insert tree in slit.

Directions for mat and napkin

For each, wash and dry remaining fabric scraps and napkin; do not use fabric softener in washer or dryer. Iron fusible web to wrong side of fabric scraps.

For mat, transfer tree pattern to paper side of web and cut 6 from Christmas print. Cut 6 (½" x ⅝") pieces from green fabric for trunks. Referring to photo, fuse trunks and trees to red felt. Draw blanket stitches around each tree and outline each trunk with red dimensional paint. Let dry. Referring to pattern, draw star at top of each tree with gold glitter dimensional paint. Let dry. Blanket-stitch around edge of mat with green floss.

For napkin, transfer tree pattern to paper side of web and cut 1 from Christmas print. Cut 1 (⅜" x ½") piece from red fabric for trunk. Referring to photo, fuse trunk and tree to 1 corner of napkin. Draw blanket stitches around tree and outline trunk with red dimensional paint. Let dry. Paint dots and dashes on edge of napkin (see photo). Let dry. Referring to pattern, draw star at top of tree with gold glitter dimensional paint. Let dry.

29

Candle Magic

Turn ordinary pillar candles into a stunning display with these quick tricks. Then decorate extra candles to give as teacher or hostess gifts.

Trees Candle

Materials

Patterns on page 51
Green paper napkin
Aleene's Paper Napkin Appliqué™ Glue
Paintbrush
3"-diameter red pillar candle
Gold glitter
Gold and silver metallic stars

Directions

Note: Be sure to test paper napkins for color-fastness as glue causes some colors to bleed.

1 Transfer patterns to green paper napkin and cut 2 small trees, 2 medium trees, and 2 large trees. Remove bottom plies of napkin to leave cutouts 1-ply thick. Working over small area at a time, brush coat of glue on candle in desired position. Press 1 tree into glue-covered area, pressing out any air bubbles. Brush coat of glue over tree. Repeat to glue remaining trees around candle, overlapping trees slightly. Let dry.

2 Working over small area at a time, brush glue over candle and trees. Sprinkle glitter onto wet glue. Let dry. Shake off excess glitter. Continue until you get desired effect. Glue 1 star at top of each tree. Let dry.

To make the Trees Candle, glue paper napkin cutouts around a candle and apply a generous amount of glitter for extra sparkle. For a table centerpiece or a mantel arrangement, decorate candles of various sizes and arrange them with bits of greenery.

Fancy Floral Candles

"I assembled this pair of candles in under an hour, so you can make them this morning and use them tonight," Heidi says. You'll need a pillar candle, Aleene's Designer Tacky Glue™, and an assortment of ribbons, charms, and other trims.

To gather your trims, check your scrap basket for bits and pieces left over from other crafting projects. Look for a single silk rose, a scrap of gold braid, or odd lengths of ribbon. Collect buttons, charms, and tiny dried flowers and use them when planning your candle decoration.

To form the base for the trims, tie a piece of ribbon in a bow around a candle. Glue decorative braid or trim on top of the ribbon, if desired.

Referring to the candles shown here for inspiration, glue the assorted trims to the bow as desired. Glue long, flat items on first and then glue on smaller, dimensional items. Let the glue dry completely before using the candle.

Keep a few pillar candles on hand (watch for holiday sales) and when you need a quick gift, embellish them with ribbons, charms, and other trims. Everyone will think you bought the candles at a fancy boutique. Only you will know how inexpensive they really were.

Teatime Tree

Heidi made the ornaments on her tea tree from brown bags and tea bags in plain white wrappers.

Materials (for 3 ornaments)

Patterns on page 51
Brown grocery bags
3" square cardboard squeegee
Aleene's Tacky Glue™
Waxed paper
Acrylic paints: red, green, white, black, yellow
Paintbrush
Toothpicks
Gold metallic thread
¼"-diameter hole punch
Tea bag in plain white wrapper
Fine-tip permanent green marker
6" length ⅜"-wide red-and-white dot grosgrain ribbon

Directions for teacup ornament

1 Cut 2 (4") squares of brown bag. Using cardboard squeegee, apply coat of glue to 1 side of 1 bag piece. With edges aligned, press remaining bag piece into glue. Transfer pattern to layered bag and cut 1 teacup. To keep ornament flat during drying, place ornament between 2 pieces of waxed paper and lay flat on table. Place a heavy book on top and let dry.

2 Referring to photo, paint 1 side of ornament, letting dry between colors. Use toothpicks to paint dots and hearts. Let dry. Cut 1 (10") length of gold thread for hanger. To attach hanger, fold gold thread in half to form loop and knot ends. Glue knot to back of ornament. Let dry.

Directions for sign ornament

1 Cut 2 (4" x 6¾") pieces of brown bag. Using cardboard squeegee, apply coat of glue to 1 side of 1 bag piece. With edges aligned, press remaining bag piece into glue. Transfer pattern to layered bag and cut 1 sign. Punch hole in ornament where indicated on pattern. To keep ornament flat during drying, place ornament between 2 pieces of waxed paper and lay flat on table. Place a heavy book on top and let dry.

2 Referring to photo, paint 1 side of ornament, letting dry between colors. Use toothpicks to paint dots. Let dry. Cut 1 (10") length of gold thread for hanger. To attach hanger, fold gold thread in half to form loop and knot ends. Thread folded end of loop through hole in ornament. Thread knotted ends through fold and pull tight to secure.

Directions for tea bag ornament

Use toothpicks to dot paint on front of tea bag for flowers and leaves (see photo). Draw tendrils with green marker (see photo). Tie ribbon in bow. Glue bow to front of tea bag below flowers. To attach hanger, fold gold thread in half to form loop and knot ends. Glue knot to back of ornament. Let dry.

Theme Trees

Give each member of your family a small tree of his or her own to decorate. Here are a few of Heidi's favorite themes.

• **Angels.** Gather angels in a variety of sizes and hang them on the tree. Add a star topper. Garland the tree with narrow strips of netting for a cloud effect.

• **Gardening.** Glue raffia bows to seed packets and add a thread hanger to each. Glue garden motif gift wrap to 1 layer of brown bag and cut out individual flowers or tools. Add a hanger to each gift wrap ornament. Wind raffia around the tree to fill in the gaps.

• **Fishing.** Use fishing line to attach fishing lures to the tree branches. (Remove the hooks from the lures first for safety.) Hang plastic worms instead of icicles.

No-Sew Stockings

These stockings are glued together, so you can add them
to your mantel in no time at all.

Materials

For each: Patterns on pages 52 and 53
Tracing paper
Pinking shears
Aleene's Tacky Glue™
Aleene's Fusible Web™
Aleene's Jewel-It™ Glue
Gold glitter dimensional paint
For tree stocking: Fabrics: 20" x 24" piece red-
  and-gold dot, green-and-gold dot scrap
15" length ⅜"-wide gold trim
Gold star charm
Red satin ribbon: 5" length ⅛"-wide, 8" length
  ½"-wide
For angel stocking: Fabrics: 24" square heavy-
  weight cream cotton; green-and-gold dot, red-
  and-gold dot, peach, and gold lamé scraps
Gold star charm
Assorted buttons
8" length ½"-wide cream satin ribbon

Directions

Note: See page 138 for tips on working with
fusible web.

1 **To make stocking pattern,** trace pattern onto
tracing paper. **For tree stocking,** extend top
edge 9½" and add ½" all around. **For angel
stocking,** extend top edge 11½" and add ½" all
around; then add ¾" to each side of stocking at
top to extend straight edge to measure 8¾".

2 **For tree stocking,** transfer stocking pattern to
red-and-gold dot fabric. Using pinking shears,
cut out; reverse pattern and cut out stocking back.
Turn under ½" at top edge of each stocking piece
and glue for hem, using Tacky Glue. On wrong
side of 1 stocking piece, squeeze line of Tacky
Glue around side and bottom edges, ½" from
edge. Do not put glue across top edge. With wrong
sides facing and edges aligned, glue stocking
pieces together. Let dry.

For angel stocking, transfer pattern to cream
fabric. Using pinking shears, cut out; reverse pattern and cut out stocking back. Fold 3" at top edge
to right side on each stocking piece and glue for
cuff, using Tacky Glue. On wrong side of 1 stocking piece, squeeze line of Tacky Glue around side
and bottom edges, ½" from edge. Do not put glue
across top edge. With wrong sides facing and edges
aligned, glue stocking pieces together. Let dry.

3 **For tree stocking,** iron fusible web to wrong
side of green-and-gold dot fabric. Transfer
tree pattern to paper side of web and cut out. Cut
tree apart along lines shown on pattern, using
pinking shears. Referring to photo, fuse tree pieces
to stocking front.

For angel stocking, iron fusible web to wrong
side of remaining fabrics. Transfer patterns to
paper side of web and cut the following: 1 toe
and 1 heel from green-and-gold dot; 1 dress and 1
sleeve from red-and-gold dot; 1 hand, 2 feet, and
1 (1"-diameter) circle for face from peach; and 1
wing from gold lamé. Referring to photo, fuse
appliqué pieces in place on stocking front.

4 **For tree stocking,** cut 1 length of trim to fit
width of each tree piece except trunk. Center
and glue braid lengths in place on tree pieces,
using Jewel-It Glue. Glue star charm at top of tree,
using Jewel-It Glue. Tie ⅛"-wide ribbon in bow.
Glue bow to trunk, using Jewel-It Glue. Let dry.
Embellish stocking front with dimensional paint
(see photo). Let dry.

For angel stocking, embellish stocking front
with dimensional paint (see photo). Glue star
charm to hand, using Jewel-It Glue. Glue buttons to
stocking front, using Jewel-It Glue. Let dry.

5 **To add hanger to each stocking,** fold ½"-
wide ribbon in half to form loop. Glue ribbon
ends inside stocking at top, using Jewel-It Glue.
Let dry.

Angel Banner

Display this no-sew decoration on your front door or over your mantel to herald the coming holiday.

Materials

Patterns on page 54

Fabrics: 23" x 36" piece white-on-white print, 18" square Christmas print, 10" x 14" piece gold lamé, 6" square yellow, 10" square peach

Aleene's Fusible Web™

Dimensional paints: peach, black, gold glitter, silver glitter

Assorted sizes gold and silver metallic stars

11" length ⅝"-wide gold ribbon

21" length ¼"-diameter wooden dowel

2 (⅝"-diameter) wooden beads

Gold metallic acrylic paint

Paintbrush

Aleene's Designer Tacky Glue™

1 yard gold metallic cording

Directions

Note: See page 138 for tips on working with fusible web.

1 Wash and dry fabrics; do not use fabric softener in washer or dryer. Fuse 1"-wide strips of fusible web to each edge on wrong side of white-on-white fabric. To hem banner, turn under 1" along both long sides and 1 short end and fuse. To make dowel casing, turn under 3" along remaining short end of fabric and fuse.

2 Iron fusible web to wrong side of remaining fabrics. To cut dress from Christmas print fabric, draw 1 triangle 22" tall and 13¼" at base on paper side of web. Cut out. Draw line across top of triangle 3¼" from tip. Cut along line and set small piece aside for another use. In same manner, draw 2 triangles 9" tall and 5" at base and cut out for sleeves.

3 Transfer patterns to paper side of web and cut 2 shoes from remaining Christmas print; 2 wings from gold lamé; 1 hair from yellow; and 2 hands, 2 feet, and 1 (5⅜"-diameter) circle for face from peach. Referring to photo for placement, fuse fabric pieces to banner.

4 Draw nostrils on face with peach dimensional paint. Draw eyes and mouth on face with black dimensional paint. Let dry. Embellish angel and draw halo and stars with gold glitter dimensional paint (see photo). While paint is still wet, press 1 gold metallic star in center of each painted star. Let dry. Draw garland with silver glitter dimensional paint (see photo). While paint is still wet, press assorted stars into garland. Let dry.

5 Tie ribbon in bow and glue to angel at neck. Let dry. Paint dowel and beads gold metallic. Let dry. Slip dowel through casing in banner. Glue 1 bead to each end of dowel. Let dry. For hanger, tie 1 end of cording to each end of dowel beside beads.

Dazzling Door Display

Make an angel on a tomato cage base for your front door and create easy fabric bows to decorate a garland and a wreath.

Tomato Cage Angel

Materials

Pattern on page 55
36" x 72" piece netting
Florist's wire: 26-gauge, 18-gauge
3-foot tall wire tomato cage
Aleene's Designer Tacky Glue™
Red plaid fabric: 1 (36" x 44") piece, 2 (18" x 20") pieces
6" x 10" piece peach felt
30" x 32½" piece gold lamé
Aleene's Fusible Web™
Batting: 14" x 31" piece, scraps
6"-diameter Battenberg lace doily
14" length ½"-wide red ribbon
6"-diameter Styrofoam ball
Serrated knife
24" square peach fabric
Yellow fake fur: 1 (4½" x 12") piece, 2 (2¼" x 12") pieces
Comb
30" length gold star garland
2 (1¼") black buttons
Fine-tip permanent black marker

Directions

1 Fold netting in thirds widthwise. Using 26-gauge florist's wire and working through all layers, run wire along 1 long edge of folded netting. Gather netting to fit top of tomato cage. Wrap netting around tomato cage about 2" from top. Twist wire ends together to secure netting. Squeeze thin line of glue on wrong side along 1 (44") edge of 36" x 44" piece of red plaid for dress. Turn under ½" and glue for hem. Let dry. Using 26-gauge florist's wire, run wire along unhemmed 44" edge of red plaid. Gather fabric to fit top of tomato cage. Wrap fabric around tomato cage on top of netting, with gathered edge of fabric about 2" from top of cage. Twist wire ends together to secure.

Aleene's front door welcomes holiday visitors. Select a fabric to match your decorating scheme when you re-create this angel for your home. If you live in an area where the winter weather is harsh, place the angel in the foyer or beside the fireplace.

2 For each sleeve, squeeze thin line of glue on wrong side along 1 (20") edge of 1 (18" x 20") piece of red plaid. Turn under ½" and glue for hem. Squeeze thin line of glue on right side along 1 (18") edge of red plaid. Overlap 18" edges and glue to make tube. Let dry. Using 26-gauge florist's wire, run wire along unhemmed 20" edge of fabric. Gather sleeve tightly. Cut 1 (36") length of 18-gauge florist's wire for arms. Slightly bend wire at center to shape. With gathered edge at top, slip 1 sleeve on each end of wire. Glue gathered edge of each sleeve to wire near bend in center of wire. Let dry. Cut 1 (5") piece of 18-gauge florist's wire. Use 5" wire length to wire arms to top of tomato cage. Glue gathered edge of sleeves and arms to dress to secure. Let dry.

3 Transfer pattern to felt and cut 4 hands. With edges aligned and wire sandwiched between, glue 2 hands together at end of each arm. Let dry.

4 Cut 2 (36") lengths of 18-gauge florist's wire for wings. Bend each wire in half to form a right angle. With right sides facing and 32½" edges aligned, fold lamé in half. Cut 4 (½" x 15") strips of fusible web. Slip web strips between lamé layers at each open edge, leaving opening in center of 32½" edge, and fuse. Turn wings right side out. Slip 14" x 31" piece of batting into wings. Place 1 prepared wire inside wings at each top corner. Glue opening closed. Let dry.

5 Cut 1 (10") length of 18-gauge florist's wire. With folded edge at top, fanfold center of wings to gather. Wrap 10" wire length around center of wings and twist ends together at top of wings to secure gathers. Form wire ends into a loop to attach wings to tomato cage. Slip wire loop over top of tomato cage at back of angel.

6 Slip edge of doily over top of tomato cage at front of angel. Tie ribbon in bow. Glue bow to doily. Let dry. Press foam ball onto top of tomato cage to form indentation. Using serrated knife, carve out indented area of foam ball to fit tomato cage. Glue scraps of batting to cover foam ball, leaving indentation uncovered. Let dry. Cover ball with peach fabric, gathering excess at bottom. Glue fabric edges inside indentation in ball, trimming to fit as needed. Let dry.

7 For hair, with right side facing face, pin 1 (12") edge of 4½" x 12" fur piece to top and sides of head to form hairline around face. Fold fur toward back of head and pin remaining edges in place. In same manner, pin 1 (2¼" x 12") fur piece in place to cover back of head. Roll remaining fur piece to form bun. Pin bun to head. Comb fur to fluff. Curve star garland into a circle for halo and glue to head. Glue button eyes in place on face. Draw mouth on face with black marker. Press head in place on angel, gluing to secure as needed. Let dry.

Wreath with Easy Fabric Bows

Heidi decorated an artificial wreath with a string of white lights, silk flowers, pinecones, baby's breath, and easy fabric bows. The ceramic angels on the wreath (positioned at 2 o'clock, 6 o'clock, and 9 o'clock) came from Germany. When Heidi was a child, the angels hung on the wall in her room, holding an organdy drape above her bed. "Every year I use these angels in one of my holiday decorations," she says. "This year I decided to use them on Mom's wreath."

The lights on this wreath are electric. Heidi ran the cord over the top of the door and down to an inside outlet. She taped the cord in place every few inches for safety. A piece of ribbon hides the cord on the door. You can use a string of battery-operated lights to avoid having to tape and hide the cord.

To make 1 fabric bow, you'll need 1 (4" x 8") strip of holiday print fabric, pinking shears, 1 (6") length and 1 (10") length of raffia, Aleene's Designer Tacky Glue™, and a button. Using the pinking shears, trim all edges of the fabric. Gather the fabric widthwise at the center of the strip. Knot 6" length of raffia around the gathered fabric to secure. Trim the excess raffia.

Tie the remaining raffia length in a bow. Glue the raffia bow to the right side of the fabric bow on top of the gathers. Glue the button on top of the raffia bow. Let dry.

Santa Wind Sock

This jolly wind sock is easy to make with fabric, fusible web, and glue. When the wind blows, Santa's ribbon beard will wave greetings to your holiday guests.

Materials

Patterns on page 55
Fabrics: 7" x 8" piece peach, pink scrap, black scrap, 4" x 11" piece and 3" x 20" strip white, 18" x 20" piece red
Aleene's Fusible Web™
Aleene's Designer Tacky Glue™
2½"-diameter red pom-pom
20" length 18-gauge florist's wire
⅞"-wide ribbon: 2 (25") lengths white, 8 (21") lengths white, 8 (19") lengths red
Jumbo rickrack: 30" length white, 19" length red
22" length ⅛"-wide red satin ribbon

Directions

Note: See page 138 for tips on working with fusible web.

1 Wash and dry fabrics; do not use fabric softener in washer or dryer. Iron fusible web to wrong side of peach, pink, black, and 4" x 11" white fabrics. Transfer patterns to paper side of web and cut 1 face from peach, 2 cheeks from pink, 2 pupils from black, and 1 mustache and 2 eyes from white.

2 Fuse ½"-wide strip of web to 1 (20") edge on wrong side of red fabric. Turn under ½" along same edge and fuse for hem. With curved edge of face ½" from hemmed edge, center and fuse face on right side of red fabric. Referring to photo, arrange cheeks, mustache, eyes, and pupils on face and fuse, leaving 2" at each end of mustache unfused. Glue pom-pom to face for nose. Let dry.

3 Squeeze thin line of glue on wrong side along each 1 (18") edge and unhemmed 20" edge of red fabric. Turn each glued edge under ½" and press into glue to hem. Squeeze thin line of glue

on right side along remaining 18" edge of red fabric. With hemmed edge on top, overlap 18" edges ½" and glue to make tube. Let dry.

4 For casing, turn top edge of tube under ½" and glue along edge, leaving 2" open to insert wire. Insert wire into casing, forming a circle. Twist ends to secure. Glue casing opening closed. Pin casing in place until glue is dry.

5 With 1 ribbon end aligned with top of face, glue 1 (25") ribbon length to each side edge of face. Glue 1 end of each remaining white ribbon to wind sock below face, trimming ribbon ends as needed to fit curve of face. Glue 1 end of each red ribbon to inside of wind sock around bottom edge at back. Pin ribbons in place until glue is dry. Notch free end of each ribbon.

6 Fuse ½"-wide strips of web along each long edge on wrong side of 3" x 20" white strip. Turn under ¾" along each long edge of strip and fuse. With 1 long edge of strip aligned with top of face, begin at back seam and glue hemmed strip around wind sock for hat trim. Pin strip in place until glue is dry.

7 Cut 1 length of white rickrack to fit bottom edge of face. Beginning and ending at back seam of wind sock, glue rickrack to wind sock, covering bottom edge of face and white ribbon ends. Beginning and ending at back seam of wind sock, glue remaining white rickrack around wind sock, covering bottom edge of white fabric strip (see photo). Beginning and ending at back seam of wind sock, glue red rickrack around top of wind sock. Pin rickrack in place until glue is dry. For hanger, glue 1 end of ⅛"-wide ribbon to inside top of wind sock at each side. Let dry.

Decorations Kids Can Make

With these directions, even kids can glue scraps of Fun Foam together to make a holiday doorknob decoration. Use small boxes to create the snowman and Santa ornaments.

Doorknob Decor

Materials
Patterns on page 56
Fun Foam: white, pink, red, green, black
Hole punches: ¼"-diameter, ⅛"-diameter
Aleene's Designer Tacky Glue™
Fine-tip permanent black marker

Directions
1 Transfer patterns to Fun Foam and cut 1 beard, 1 mustache, 1 hat trim, and 1 hat pompom from white; 1 face from pink; 1 hat from red; and 1 base from green. Punch ¼" circle from remaining red for nose. Punch 2 (⅛") circles from black for eyes.

2 Referring to photo, glue foam pieces to base to form Santa. Let dry. Add lettering with black marker.

Box Ornaments

Materials (for both)

For each: Patterns on page 57
Aleene's Designer Tacky Glue™
1 (10") length gold metallic thread
For snowman: Black paper scrap
24" length ⅛"-wide red satin ribbon
2" square white box (See note below.)
3 (¼") half-round black beads
Pom-poms: 1 (2"-diameter) white, 2 (½"-
    diameter) green, 1 (¼"-diameter) red
2 (¼") wiggle eyes
1 (⅜" x 9") strip gold-and-green dot fabric
Pearl-headed florist's pin
For Santa: Red, white, and black felt scraps
Black Fun Foam scrap
1 (¼" x 6⅛") strip black paper
2" x 2½" x 1" gift box, wrapped with red paper
Pom-poms: 1 (1½"-diameter) pink, 1 (¾"-
    diameter) white, 1 (¼"-diameter) red
2 (¼"-diameter) half-round black beads
¾" yellow plastic star

Directions for snowman

Note: If you cannot find a white box, wrap box with white paper to use for snowman's body.

1 Transfer hat brim pattern to black paper and cut out. Cut slits in hat brim where indicated on pattern. From remaining black paper, cut 1 (1½" x 4½") strip for hat crown. Roll hat crown to form a tube. Overlap ends and glue. Let dry. Center and glue crown on brim. Let dry. From ribbon, cut 1 (4") length and 1 (20") length. Glue 4" ribbon around hat for trim, overlapping ribbon ends. Let dry.

2 Wrap 20" ribbon around box as if wrapping a package. Glue ends to box. Let dry. Glue half-round beads to ribbon on front of box for buttons. Let dry. Center and glue white pom-pom on top of ribbon ends for head. Let dry.

3 Glue green pom-poms to head for ear muffs. Glue red pom-pom nose and wiggle eyes to face. Let dry. Wrap fabric strip around neck and glue in place. Let dry. Glue hat to head. To attach hanger, fold gold thread in half to form loop and knot ends. Push point of pin through thread at loop end of hanger. Push pin into head through hat.

Directions for Santa

1 Transfer patterns to felt and cut 1 hat and 2 arms from red, 1 mustache and 1 beard from white, and 2 hands from black. From remaining white felt, cut 1 (½" x 5") strip for hat trim. Transfer feet pattern to Fun Foam and cut out.

2 To attach hanger, fold gold thread in half to form loop and knot ends. Curve hat into a cone shape, overlapping straight edges and catching knot of hanger in hat tip, and glue. Glue white felt strip around bottom of hat for trim. Let dry.

3 Centering strip lengthwise on body, glue paper strip around box for belt. Glue feet to 1 end of box. Glue pink pom-pom to opposite end of box. Glue hat to head. Glue white pom-pom to hat tip. Glue red pom-pom nose and bead eyes to face. Let dry. Referring to photo, glue remaining felt pieces in place on Santa. Glue star to Santa's hands. Let dry.

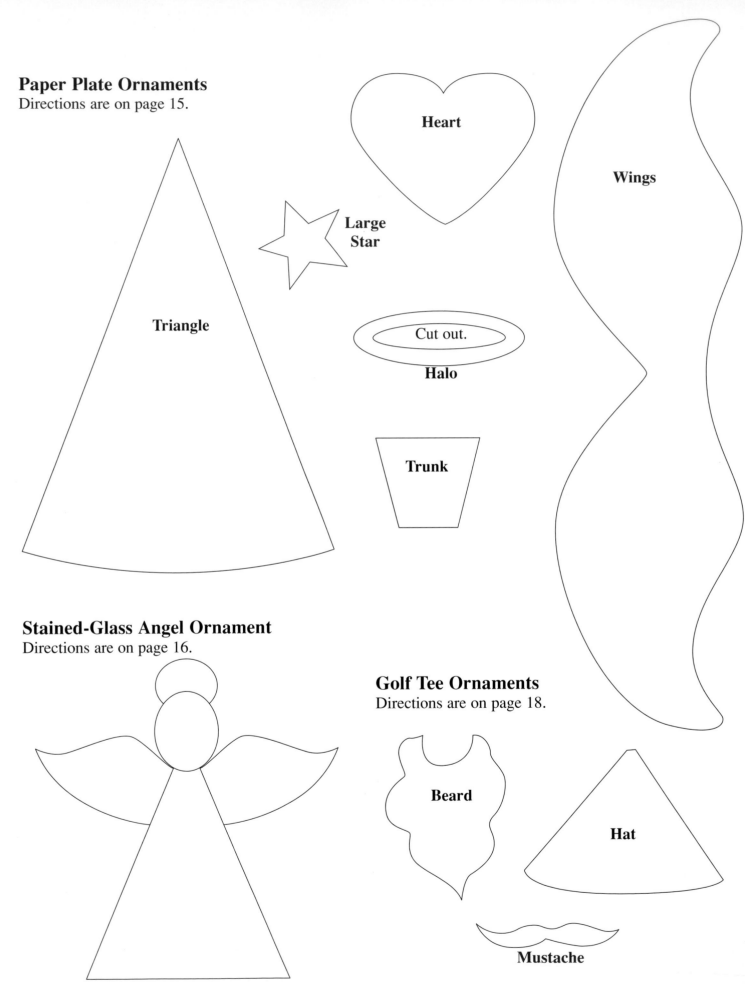

Paper Plate Ornaments
Directions are on page 15.

Heart

Large Star

Triangle

Wings

Cut out.

Halo

Trunk

Stained-Glass Angel Ornament
Directions are on page 16.

Golf Tee Ornaments
Directions are on page 18.

Beard

Hat

Mustache

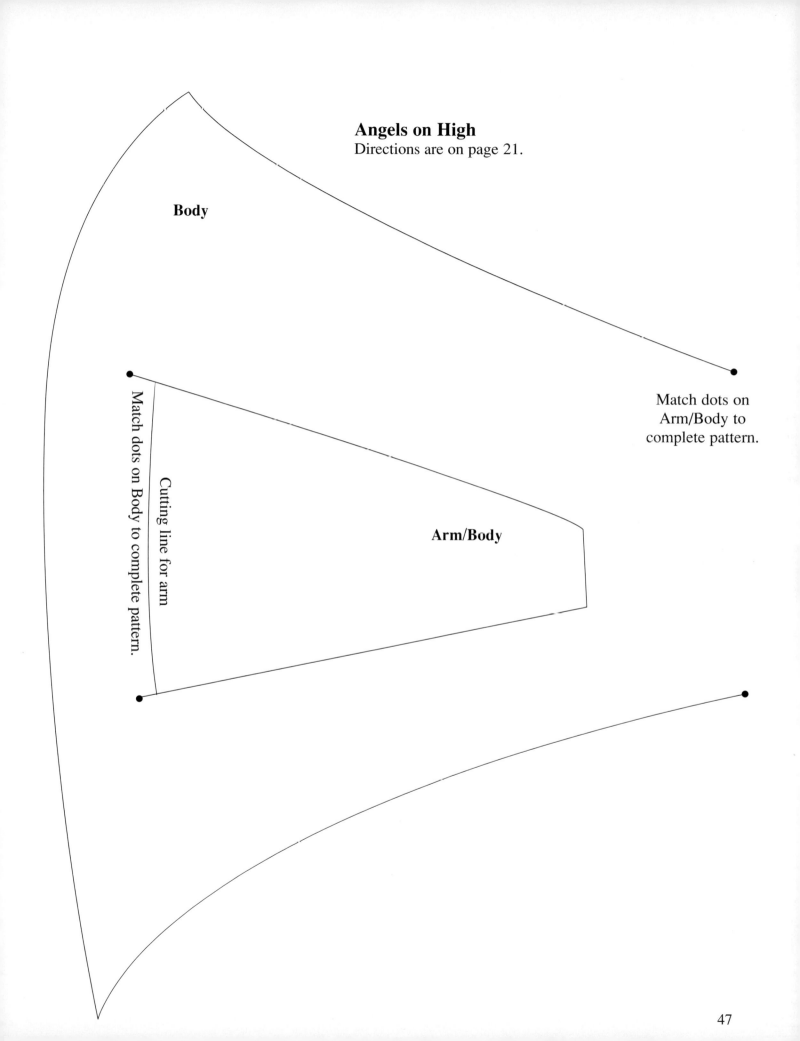

Angels on High
Directions are on page 21.

Body

Match dots on Arm/Body to complete pattern.

Match dots on Body to complete pattern.

Cutting line for arm

Arm/Body

Burnt Brown Bag Reindeer
Directions are on page 22.

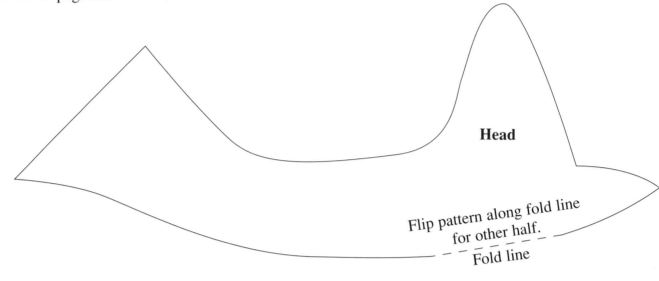

Head

Flip pattern along fold line
for other half.
Fold line

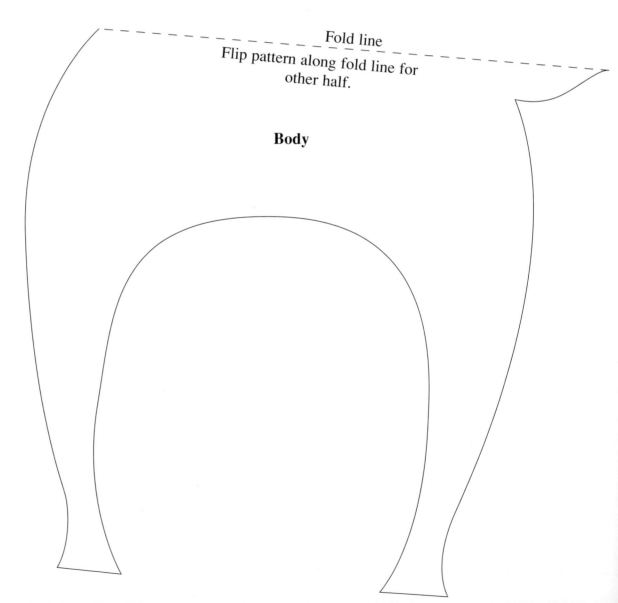

Fold line
Flip pattern along fold line for
other half.

Body

Glittering Glue Snowflakes
Directions are on page 24.

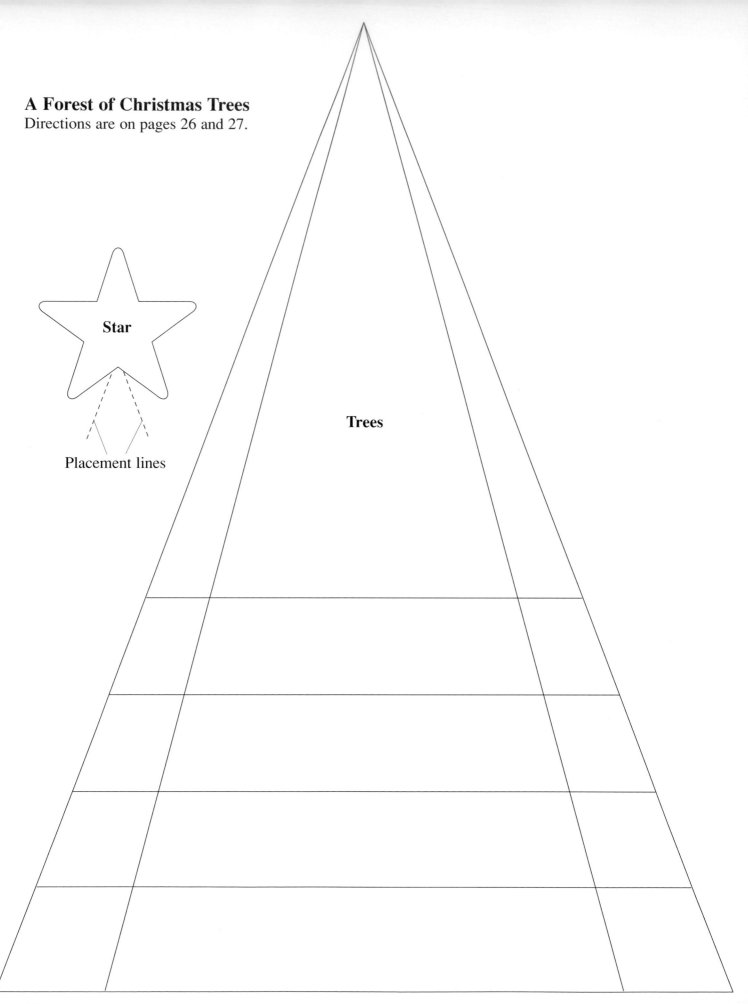

A Forest of Christmas Trees
Directions are on pages 26 and 27.

Star

Placement lines

Trees

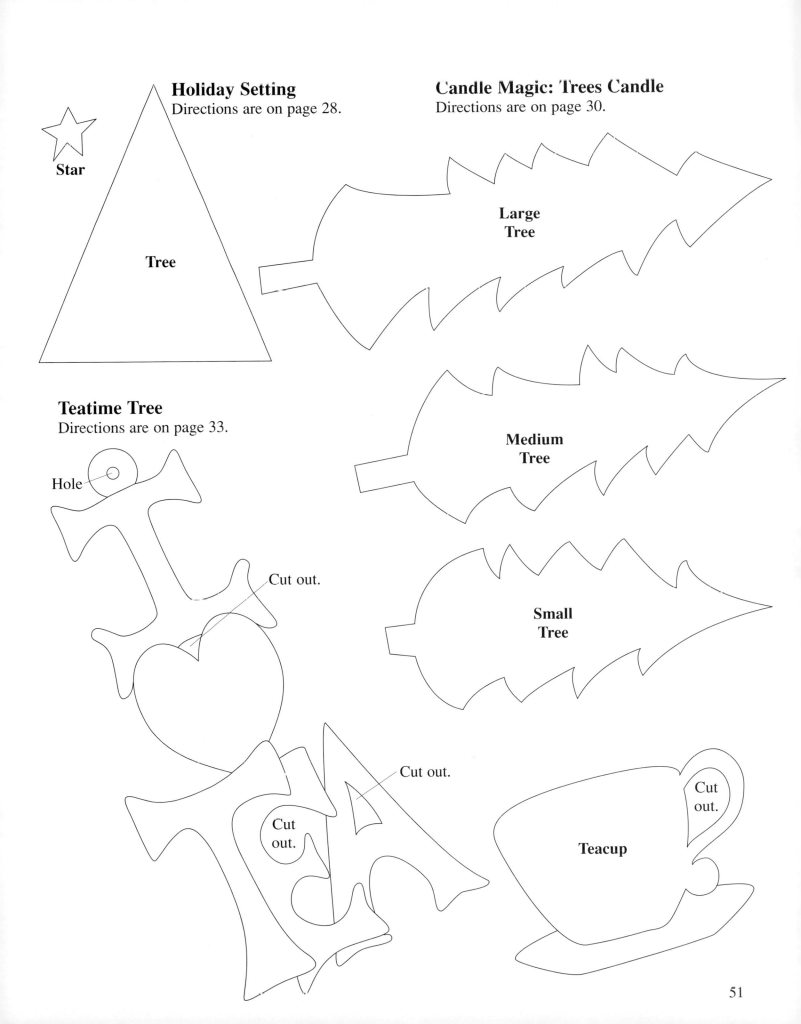

Star

Holiday Setting
Directions are on page 28.

Tree

Candle Magic: Trees Candle
Directions are on page 30.

Large Tree

Medium Tree

Small Tree

Teatime Tree
Directions are on page 33.

Hole

Cut out.

Cut out.

Cut out.

Cut out.

Cut out.

Teacup

51

No-Sew Stockings
Directions are on page 34.

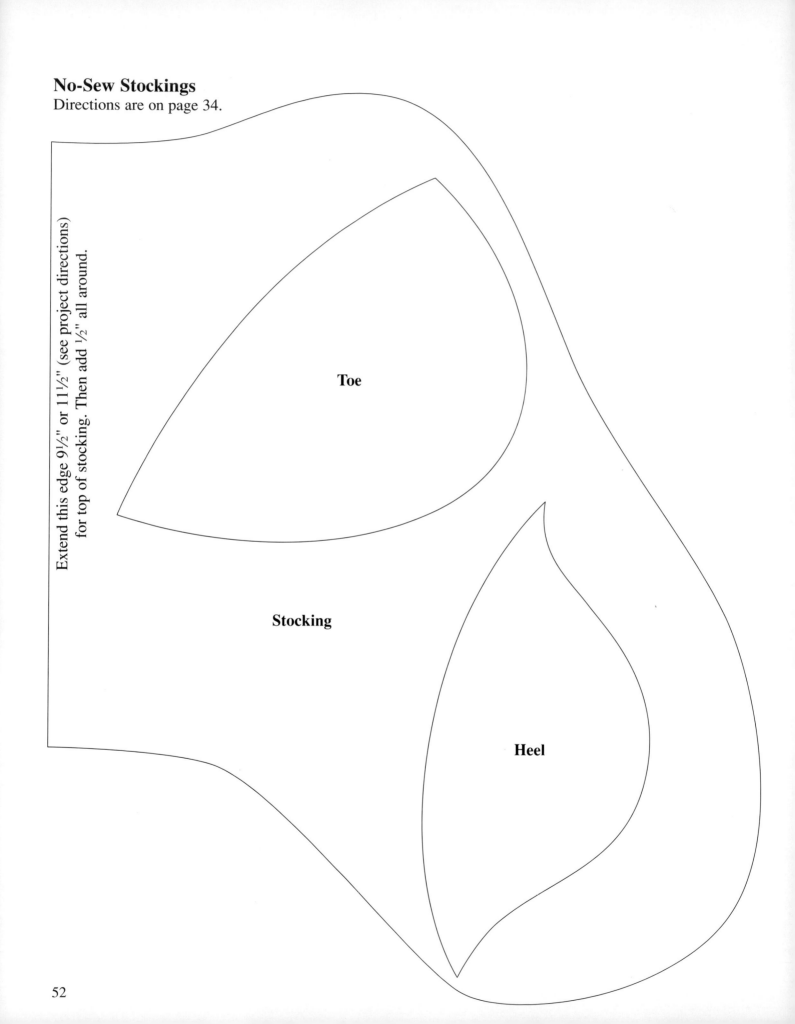

Extend this edge 9½" or 11½" (see project directions) for top of stocking. Then add ½" all around.

Toe

Stocking

Heel

No-Sew Stockings
Directions are on page 34.

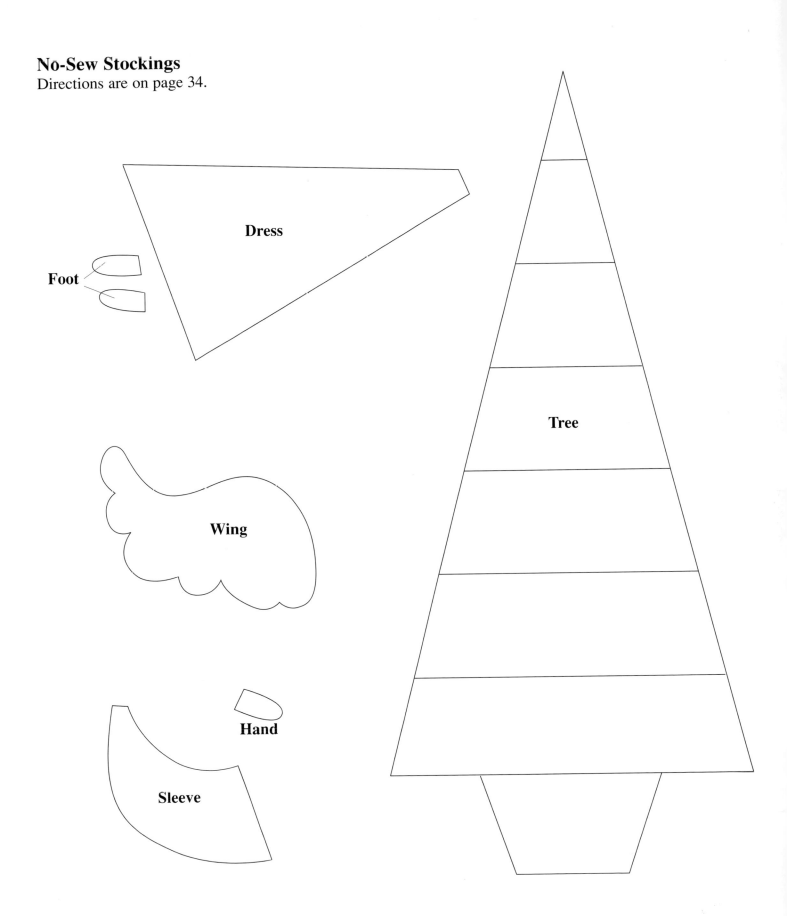

Dress

Foot

Wing

Hand

Sleeve

Tree

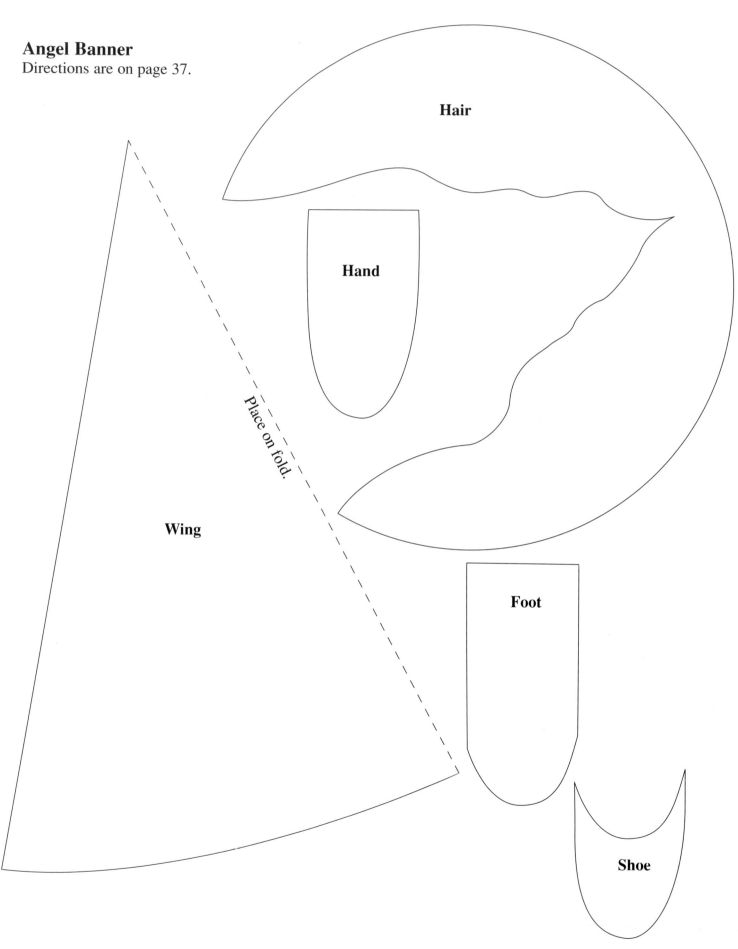

Angel Banner
Directions are on page 37.

Hair

Hand

Place on fold.

Wing

Foot

Shoe

Dazzling Door Display: Tomato Cage Angel

Directions are on pages 39 and 40.

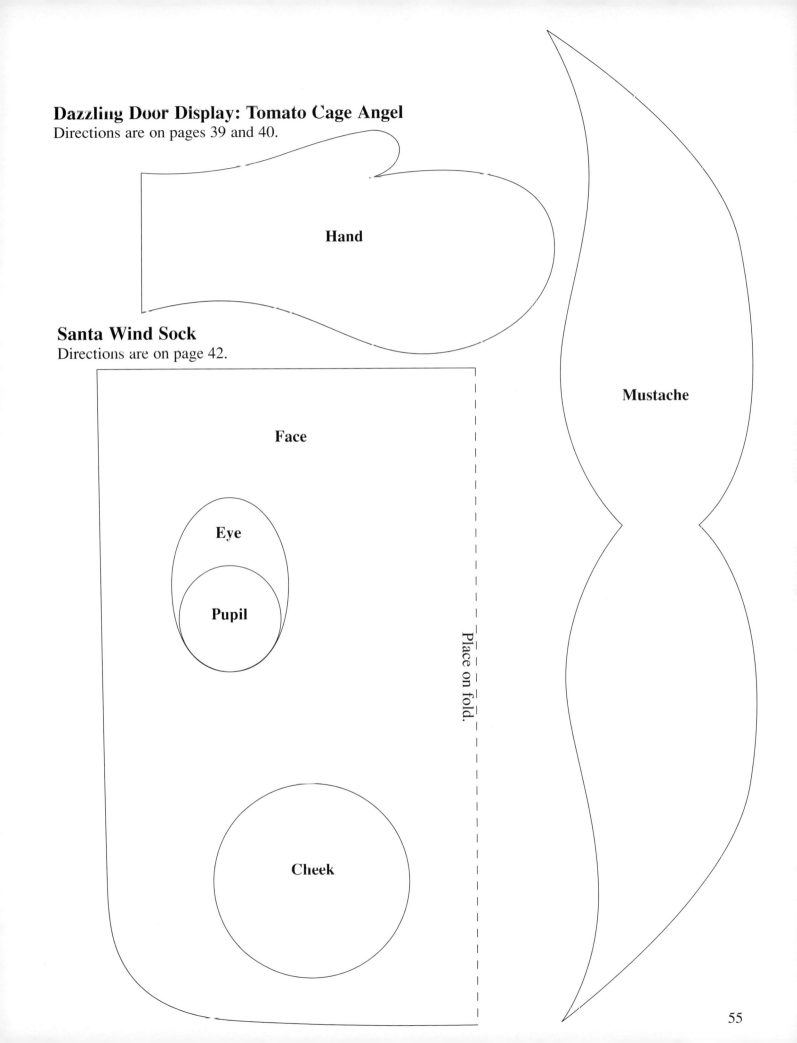

Hand

Santa Wind Sock

Directions are on page 42.

Face

Eye

Pupil

Cheek

Place on fold.

Mustache

Decorations Kids Can Make:
Doorknob Decor
Directions are on page 44.

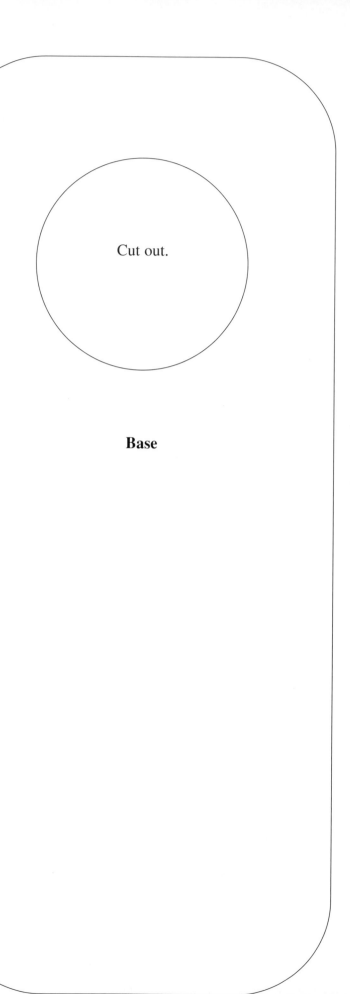

Cut out.

Base

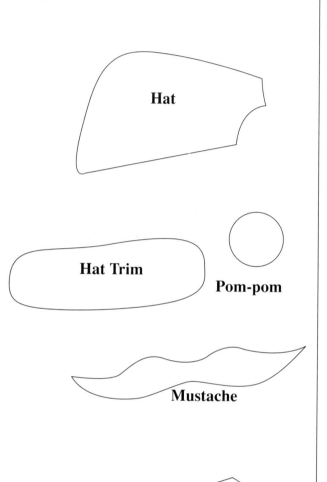

Hat

Hat Trim

Pom-pom

Mustache

Face

Beard

Decorations Kids Can Make:
Box Ornaments
Directions are on page 45.

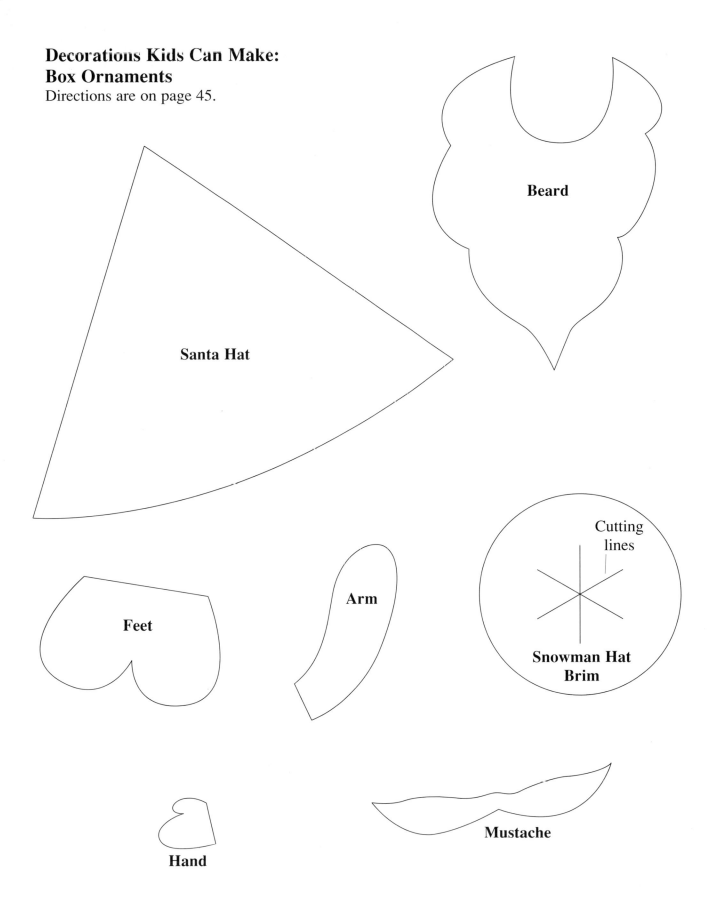

Santa Hat

Beard

Feet

Arm

Cutting
lines

Snowman Hat
Brim

Hand

Mustache

To: Julie
From: Brad

Baked Just For You!
To Mom
From Heidi

Tiffany

Crafty Holiday Gifts

Here, you'll find a wide selection of ideas for handmade gifts as well as quick-and-easy wraps and tags. You can also craft unique cards to send your holiday greetings to friends and family.

Jewelry Box

Craft a fabric-covered jewelry box for your sister or mother. Costume jewelry is a good source for the trims glued to the box lid.

Materials

Gift box with lid
Batting (See Step 1 for amount needed.)
Fabric (See Step 1 for amount needed.)
Aleene's Designer Tacky Glue™
4 (¾"-diameter) wooden beads
28" length ⅛"-wide satin ribbon
6" length 26-gauge florist's wire
Assorted trims: buttons, gold charms, beads, pearls, ribbon roses

Directions

1 Cut into corners on 1 side of box lid to allow for hinged top. Measure width and length, including rim of box lid. Cut 1 piece of batting to these measurements. Add ¾" all around and cut 1 piece of fabric to these measurements. Measure depth and around sides of box. Cut 1 piece of batting to these measurements. Add ½" to length and 1" to width and cut 1 piece of fabric to these measurements.

2 Glue batting to right side of box lid. Glue batting around box sides. Let dry. Lay fabric for lid right side down on work surface. Center box lid, batting side down, on fabric. Fold excess fabric to inside of lid and glue, clipping edges at hinge side of lid and corners as needed. Let dry. Center and glue fabric strip around sides of box. Overlap ends of fabric, turn top end under ¼", and glue. Fold excess fabric over top and bottom edges of box, clipping corners as needed, and glue. Let dry.

3 Glue 1 bead to each bottom corner of box. Let dry. Place lid on box. Glue hinge side of box lid to 1 side of box. Let dry. Referring to pages 142 and 143, make multilooped bow with ribbon and florist's wire. Trim wire ends. Glue bow and assorted trims to box lid as desired (see photo). Let dry.

Fabric Frames

Dress up an old frame with a tube of gathered fabric.
Select fabrics to complement a room's decor or to
follow the theme of a photograph.

Materials (for 1 frame)

Wooden picture frame
2 complementary fabrics (See Step 1 for amount
   needed.)
Aleene's No-Sew Fabric Glue™ or thread to match
   fabric and needle
3" square cardboard squeegee
Aleene's Designer Tacky Glue™
Assorted trims: silk flowers, buttons, charms
Aleene's Stick Glue™

Directions

1 Remove backing and glass from frame and set
   aside. Measure perimeter of frame. Multiply
measurement by 3. Measure depth of frame. Add
1½" to this measurement. Cut 1 strip to these
measurements from 1 fabric. Using frame backing
as guide, cut 1 piece from complementary fabric to
cover right side of frame backing.

2 Squeeze line of No-Sew Glue on wrong side
   of fabric strip along each short end. Turn
under ½" at each short end and press into glue for
hem. Let dry. To make fabric tube, squeeze line of
No-Sew Glue on right side of fabric strip along 1
long edge. With right sides facing and raw edges
aligned, fold fabric in half lengthwise and press
into glue. Let dry. (*Note:* If desired, you may stitch
fabric tube instead of gluing it.) Turn fabric tube
right side out.

3 Carefully pull frame apart at 1 corner. Slip
   fabric tube on frame. Glue frame corner
together, using Designer Tacky Glue. Let dry.
Arrange fabric gathers around frame as desired,
overlapping ends.

4 Use cardboard squeegee to apply No-Sew
   Glue to frame backing. Glue fabric to right
side of backing. Let dry. Using Designer Tacky

Glue, glue assorted trims to frame as desired. Let
dry. Place photo onto fabric-covered backing and
glue, using stick glue. Place backing into frame.

Dresser Tray

Cardboard shapes and glue embossing give this
dresser tray loads of texture and design. Surprise
Dad with a gift to help him keep track of his keys
and coins on his dresser.

Materials

2 (½-gallon) cardboard milk cartons
Aleene's Designer Tacky Glue™
Clothespins
Assorted cardboard shapes (See note below.)
Black acrylic paint
Paintbrush
Gold paste paint
4 (1"-diameter) wooden beads

Directions

Note: Heidi purchased a bag of assorted cardboard shapes. If you are unable to find precut
shapes, simply cut shapes from cardboard as
desired to decorate your dresser tray.

1 Draw line around each milk carton, 2" from
bottom. Cut off top part of each carton and set
aside for another use. Glue cartons together side
by side. Use clothespins to hold cartons together
until glue is dry.

2 Glue cardboard shapes to sides of dresser tray
as desired. Let dry. Apply dots and lines of
glue to cardboard shapes and dresser tray as
desired (see photo). Let dry. Paint entire dresser
tray and beads black. Let dry.

3 To add gold highlights, rub finger in gold
paste paint, wipe off excess paint on paper
towel, and gently rub finger over dresser tray.
Continue adding gold to each piece until you get
desired effect. Let dry. Glue 1 bead to each bottom
corner of dresser tray.

Stained-Glass Box

Apply gold foil and bits of red and green paper napkins to a glass box to create this elegant accessory.

Materials
Pattern on page 94
White paper
Decorative glass box
Aleene's 3-D Foiling™ Glue
Gold press-and-peel craft foil
Rubber pencil grip (optional)
Green and red 1-ply sheer paper napkins or tissue paper
½" shader or sponge paintbrush
Aleene's Reverse Collage™ Glue

Directions
Note: Test paper napkins or tissue paper for colorfastness by applying glue to a scrap of paper.

1 Center and transfer tree pattern on white paper. Trim paper to within ½" of design. Working over 1 design area at a time, tape pattern in place on inside of box lid. Using 3-D Foiling Glue, trace pattern onto outside of box lid (see photo). Apply dots of glue within tree outline for ornaments. Remove pattern. In same manner, trace additional trees onto box lid. Let glue dry for about 24 hours. (Glue will be opaque and sticky when dry. Glue must be thoroughly dry before foil is applied.)

2 To apply gold foil, lay foil dull side down on top of glue lines. Using fingers or pencil grip, gently but firmly press foil onto glue, completely covering glue with foil. Be sure to press foil into crevices. Peel away foil paper. If any part of glue lines is not covered, reapply foil as needed.

3 For each tree, transfer pattern to green paper napkin and cut out, adding ¼" all around. Crumple napkin tree and then flatten it, leaving some wrinkles. Working over 1 design area at a time, brush coat of Reverse Collage Glue on inside of box lid in desired position. Press napkin piece into glue-covered area. Working from outside edges to center, use fingers or brush to gently

wrinkle napkin, shaping it to fit design area. Brush coat of Reverse Collage Glue on top of napkin.

4 For trees border, tear red paper napkin into odd-shaped pieces. Refer to Step 3 to apply napkin pieces to box lid, overlapping them for added dimension, until you get desired effect. Let dry.

5 Referring to steps 1 and 2, apply 3-D Foiling Glue and gold foil in geometric patterns to each side of box (see photo). Referring to Step 3 and photo for colors, cut and glue napkin pieces to decorate each side of box. Let dry.

Collage Frame

With these directions, turn a large picture frame into a fancy collage frame. Choose any number of photos and use gold foiling to border each one.

Materials

Large picture frame
Collage mat to fit frame (optional)
Aleene's 3-D Foiling™ Glue
Gold press-and-peel craft foil
Rubber pencil grip (optional)
Fabric to cover work surface
Assorted colors tissue paper
½" shader or sponge paintbrush
Aleene's Reverse Collage™ Glue

Directions

Note: Test tissue paper for colorfastness by applying glue to a scrap of paper.

1 Remove backing and glass from frame and set frame and backing aside. Arrange photos right side down on 1 side of glass and tape in place. Lay glass on work surface with photos right side up. (If desired, lay collage mat under glass instead of photos and use for pattern.) Using 3-D Foiling Glue, draw decorative designs and border for each photo on glass (see photo). Let glue dry for about 24 hours. (Glue will be opaque and sticky when dry. Glue must be thoroughly dry before foil is applied.) Remove photos from glass.

2 To apply gold foil, lay foil dull side down on top of glue lines. Using fingers or pencil grip, gently but firmly press foil onto glue, completely covering glue with foil. Be sure to press foil into crevices. Peel away foil paper. If any part of glue lines is not covered, reapply foil as needed.

3 Cover work surface with fabric to protect foiling. Lay glass, foil side down, on fabric. Cut assorted colors of tissue paper into pieces slightly larger than border design areas (see photo). Crumple each paper piece and then flatten it, leaving some wrinkles. Working over 1 design area at a time, brush coat of Reverse Collage Glue on glass in desired position. Press paper piece into glue-covered area. Working from outside edges to center, use fingers or brush to gently wrinkle paper, shaping it to fit design area. Brush coat of Reverse Collage Glue on top of paper. In same manner, apply paper pieces to all design areas (see photo).

4 For background areas of glass, tear 1 color of tissue paper into odd-shaped pieces. (*Note:* Do not apply tissue paper to areas where photos will be placed.) Crumple each paper piece and then flatten it, leaving some wrinkles. Working over small area at a time, brush coat of Reverse Collage Glue on glass in desired position. Press paper piece into glue-covered area. Brush coat of Reverse Collage Glue on top of paper, wrinkling paper to add texture. In same manner, apply additional paper pieces, overlapping them for added dimension, until desired effect is achieved. Let dry.

5 Cut piece of tissue paper 1" larger all around than frame backing. Crumple tissue paper and then flatten it, leaving some wrinkles. Brush coat of Reverse Collage Glue on frame backing. Press paper into glue. Brush coat of Reverse Collage Glue on top of paper, wrinkling paper to add texture. Let dry. Arrange photos on wrong side of glass and tape in place. Place glass and backing in frame.

Mosaic Vase

Use tissue paper to decorate an inexpensive plastic bottle. Fill the vase with an arrangement of flowers in colors to match the paper.

Materials

Plastic bottle with geometric pattern
Assorted colors tissue paper
Aleene's Paper Napkin Appliqué™ Glue
½" shader paintbrush
Clear spray sealer
Trims: embroidery floss, metallic yarns and thread, specialty yarns, assorted beads

Directions

Note: Test tissue paper for colorfastness by applying glue to a scrap of paper.

1 Cut pieces of tissue paper to fit areas of geometric pattern on bottle. Working over small area at a time, brush coat of glue on bottle. Press paper pieces into glue-covered area. Brush coat of glue over tissue paper. Continue until surface of bottle is covered. Let dry.

2 Apply 1 coat of spray sealer to bottle. Let dry. Handling all lengths as 1, knot floss, yarns, and thread around bottle neck. Thread beads on streamers as desired, knotting to secure.

Pretty Plant Pokes

Butterfly plant pokes will add a handmade touch to a gift of flowers or a potted plant. You can also wire these butterflies to a wreath for a door decoration.

Materials (for 3 plant pokes)
Patterns on page 94
Aleene's Clear Shrink-It™ Plastic
Dimensional paints: black, white
Toothpick
6 (1") lengths gold metallic thread
Assorted colors paper napkins or tissue paper
Aleene's Reverse Collage Glue™
Paintbrush
3 (10") lengths 22-gauge florist's wire
Needlenose pliers

Directions
Note: Test paper napkins or tissue paper for colorfastness by applying glue to a scrap of paper.

1 **For each butterfly,** trace desired pattern onto Shrink-It with dimensional paint. Draw wing details and fill in butterfly body with paint. Using toothpick, press 1 end each of 2 lengths of gold thread into wet paint at top of head for antennae.

Let dry. Cut out butterfly, cutting close to paint line.

2 Referring to photo and pattern, cut or tear pieces of tissue paper or paper napkins slightly larger than design areas of wings. Crumple 1 paper piece and then flatten it, leaving some wrinkles. Working over 1 design area at a time, brush coat of glue on wrong side of butterfly in desired position. Press paper piece into glue-covered area. Brush coat of glue on top of paper, wrinkling paper to add texture. In same manner, apply additional paper pieces until you get desired effect. Let dry.

3 Using pliers, bend over 1" at 1 end of 1 wire to form butterfly body support. Press bent area of wire tightly to wire. Lay butterfly wrong side up on work surface. Place bent area of wire on body area of butterfly. To attach butterfly to wire, fill in butterfly body area with dimensional paint, covering wire. Let dry.

Sachet Ornaments

Make lots of these sweetly scented gift ornaments for the charity bazaar—they'll sell quickly.

Materials (for 1 sachet ornament)
2 (3½" x 3¾") pieces print fabric
Aleene's Fusible Web™
1 (2½" x 2¾") piece thin batting
Essential oil
Assorted trims (See photo.)
Aleene's Designer Tacky Glue™
1 (10") length gold metallic thread

Directions

1 Fuse ½"-wide strips of fusible web to each edge on wrong side of 1 fabric piece. Center batting on wrong side of fused piece. Place a few drops of essential oil on batting. With wrong sides facing and raw edges aligned, place remaining piece of fabric on top of batting. Fuse fabric layers together.

2 Referring to photo for inspiration, glue trims to ornament as desired. Let dry. For hanger, fold gold thread in half to form loop and knot ends. Glue knot to top back of ornament. Let dry.

Embellished Glass Ornaments

Add glittery stars or simple dots of paint to a purchased ornament for a super-quick gift for a hostess or a teacher. Make the hanger with a dressy bow and pretty beads.

Materials (for 2 ornaments)
Pattern on page 94
Glass ball ornaments: 1 gold, 1 teal
Gold dimensional paint
Aleene's Tacky Glue™
Small round paintbrush
Gold fine glitter
1 (24") length each gold-mesh and teal ribbon
2 (6") lengths 26-gauge florist's wire
2 (12") lengths gold metallic thread
Assorted beads

Directions

1 **For gold ornament,** dot gold paint on ornament as desired. Let dry.

   For teal ornament, transfer star pattern to ornament as many times as desired. Pour small puddle of glue into a container. Add a little water to thin glue. Brush glue on ornament inside marked line of 1 star. To hide marked lines, brush glue over them. Sprinkle generous amount of glitter into wet glue and let dry. Shake off excess glitter. Repeat to apply glue and glitter to each star on ornament.

2 **For each ornament,** referring to pages 142 and 143, make multilooped bow with 1 ribbon length and 1 length of florist's wire. Use tails of wire to attach bow to hanger on matching ornament. For beaded hanging loop, thread 1 length of gold thread through ornament hanger. Fold thread in half. String assorted beads on both thread ends as desired. Knot thread after last bead to secure. Knot thread ends, leaving a 2½" to 3" loop for hanger.

Holiday Coaster Set

These handy coasters are fun for your home or for holiday gifts. A layer of Shrink-It inside each coaster protects furniture from moisture.

Materials (for 1 set)

Patterns on page 94
1 (½-gallon) cardboard milk carton
Aleene's Designer Tacky Glue™
Fabrics: 1 (6" x 16") strip holly print, 1 (4¼") square holly print, 4 (4¼") squares white, assorted Christmas print and holly print scraps
1 (17¼") length red jumbo rickrack
Cardboard: 1 (3¾") square, 4 (3½") squares
4 (3½") squares Aleene's Opake Shrink-It™ Plastic
Aleene's Fusible Web™
⅝"-square sponge piece
Acrylic paints: red, green
Fine-tip permanent black marker

Directions

1 **For holder,** draw line around milk carton, 2" from bottom. Cut off top part of carton and set aside for another use. Center and cut 1 (1½" x 2") opening on 1 side of carton for front of holder (see photo). With 1 long edge of holly print strip extending 1" beyond bottom of container, glue strip around sides of container. Overlap ends of fabric, turn top end under ¼", and glue. Cut opening in fabric at front of holder, leaving ½" all around. Turn edges under around opening and glue. Fold excess fabric to bottom and inside of container and glue. Let dry.

2 Starting at 1 side of opening and with edge of rickrack extending beyond edge of container, glue rickrack inside container around top edge (see photo). Let dry.

3 Center and glue 3¾" cardboard square on wrong side of 4¼" holly print square. Fold excess fabric to cardboard and glue. Glue covered cardboard inside container. Let dry.

4 **For each coaster,** center and stack 1 Shrink-It square and 1 (3½") cardboard square on wrong side of 1 white fabric square. Fold excess fabric to cardboard and glue. Let dry. Iron fusible web to wrong side of fabric scraps. Transfer star or heart pattern to paper side of web and cut out. Center and fuse cutout on right side of white fabric.

5 Dip ⅝"-square sponge into water and wring out excess water. Pour puddle of paint onto waxed paper. Dip sponge into paint and blot excess paint on paper towel. Press sponge onto right side of coaster to paint border (see photo). Let dry. Outline fused appliqué and border squares with black marker.

Gifts Kids Can Make

Help your child get started on crafting decoupaged soap and a decorated basket for Grandma, a hardware frame for Grandpa, or a quick bookmark for a teacher.

Basket & Decorated Soaps

Materials (for 1 basket and 1 soap)

For basket: 5" x 6" x 1½" basket

White spray paint

Aleene's Designer Tacky Glue™

1 (19") length each 2½"-wide, 2"-wide, and 1⅛"-wide white pregathered lace trim

Variegated wire-edged ribbon: 1 yard 1"-wide pink, 16" length 1"-wide green

For decorated soap: Aleene's Instant Decoupage Glue™

Decoupage print or gift wrap cutouts

1 bar soap

Paintbrush

Directions

1 **For basket,** spray-paint basket white. Let dry. Use Designer Tacky Glue to assemble basket. With bound edge aligned with bottom of basket, glue lace lengths around sides of basket, beginning with widest piece. Pin lace in place until glue is dry.

2 To make 1 bow for each short end of basket, cut 1 (8") length of pink ribbon. Tie ribbon in bow. Center and glue 1 bow on basket at each short end. To make 1 ribbon flower, cut 1 (6") length of pink ribbon. Squeeze line of glue along 1 long edge of ribbon. Beginning at 1 end, roll ribbon, gathering bottom edge and pinching together to form flower. Pin gathered edge of flower until glue is dry. Repeat to make 2 more flowers.

3 To make 1 ribbon leaf, cut 1 (3") length of green ribbon. Fold down ribbon ends, overlapping edges slightly to form leaf (see photo). Pinch bottom of leaf together to shape. Repeat to make 4 more leaves. Center and glue ribbon leaves and flowers on basket front (see photo). Pin leaves and flowers in place until glue is dry.

4 **For 1 decorated soap,** use Decoupage Glue to apply cutouts to soap. Brush coat of glue on soap in desired position. Press 1 cutout into glue-covered area and use fingers to press out any air bubbles. Brush coat of glue on top of cutout, covering edges of paper. In same manner, apply additional cutouts to soap until you get desired effect. Let dry. Brush second coat of glue on top of cutouts. Let dry.

Hardware Picture Frame

Materials
Picture frame
Waxed paper
Assorted hardware (See photo.)
Aleene's Designer Tacky Glue™
Acrylic paints: black, metallic copper, blue-green, green, white
Paintbrush
Small sponge piece

Directions
1 Remove backing and glass from frame and set aside. Cover work surface with waxed paper. Lay frame right side up on waxed paper. Glue hardware to frame as desired. Let dry.

2 Paint frame black, covering all hardware pieces. Let dry. Sponge-paint frame with copper, blue-green, green, and white paints, letting dry between colors. Put glass and backing into frame.

Bookmarks

Materials (for 1 bookmark)
Fine-tip permanent black marker
Aleene's Clear Shrink-It™ Plastic
Aleene's Paper Napkin Appliqué™ Glue
Paintbrush
Gift wrap or greeting card cutout
Waxed paper
Rolling pin or brayer

Directions
1 Using black marker, draw 1 (2" x 6") rectangle on 1 side of Shrink-It. Brush coat of glue on Shrink-It in desired position for cutout. Press cutout right side down into glue-covered area and use fingers to press out any air bubbles. Brush coat of glue on top of cutout, covering edges.

2 Cut 1 (3" x 7") piece of waxed paper. Crumple waxed paper tightly and then flatten it, leaving some wrinkles. Brush coat of glue inside marked line. Press waxed paper into glue-covered area. Use rolling pin or brayer to firmly press waxed paper into glue, pressing out any air bubbles. Let dry.

3 Cut out bookmark, cutting just inside marked line and rounding corners or cutting 1 short end to form a point (see photo).

Stamp-a-Wrap

Make a set of simple foam stamps to create unique gift wrap or to add a personal touch to a gift bag.

Materials (for making stamp)
Patterns on page 95
Fun Foam
Foam-core board scrap
Aleene's Designer Tacky Glue™
Acrylic paints in desired colors
Paintbrush

Directions

Note: Use Fun Foam stamps on white or kraft paper to make gift wrap and on heavyweight paper or card stock to make tags or cards. Decorate a purchased bag with a stamped design for a super-quick gift wrap.

1 Transfer desired pattern to Fun Foam and cut out. Center and glue foam cutouts on foam-core board scrap, leaving space between pieces as indicated on pattern. Let dry. Trim edges of foam core to within 1" of design.

2 Paint foam stamp with desired color of acrylic paint. Position stamp on printing surface and press firmly, being sure all areas of stamp come into contact with printing surface. (*Hint:* It is a good idea to practice on a piece of scrap paper to determine correct amount of pressure and paint needed to get desired effect.) Apply fresh coat of paint to stamp and reapply to printing surface as desired. Let dry. To apply different color of paint to stamp, let paint on stamp dry and then apply new color. To use several colors on same stamp, paint each area of foam cutout with desired color. (*Hint:* To print on roll of paper, unroll several feet of paper and print with design as desired. Let dry. Roll up printed portion and unroll next section of paper.)

Block-print bright packages on white paper for this easy gift wrap. Make matching cards or tags to complement the wrap.

Once you've created the simple stamps, print holiday designs on purchased gift bags for last-minute wraps. Let your children help make the gift wraps to get everyone in the holiday spirit.

Gifts of Good Taste

Heidi offers three ideas for presenting tasty gifts this season. Place cookies or snacks in one of the boxes or wrap a loaf of bread with holiday print fabric.

Trees Box

Materials

Patterns on pages 95 and 96
Round papier-mâché box with lid (4½" high and 9" in diameter)
Gold spray paint
Natural sea sponge
Acrylic paints: green, white
Waxed paper
1"-square sponge piece
Fabric: 1 (6" x 8") piece green, 1 (10") square green star print
Aleene's Fusible Web™
Aleene's Designer Tacky Glue™
10 gold metallic star sequins
Gold dimensional paint

Directions

1 Spray-paint box and lid gold. Let dry. Dip sea sponge into water and wring out excess water. Pour separate small puddles of green and white paint onto waxed paper. Dip sponge into green paint and blot excess paint on paper towel. Gently press sponge onto sides of box until you get desired effect. Let dry. Repeat with white paint. In same manner, sponge-paint top of box lid. Dip 1"-square sponge into water and wring out excess water. Dip sponge into green paint and blot excess paint on paper towel. Press sponge onto rim of box lid. Skip 1" of rim and press sponge onto lid again. Repeat to paint green squares around rim of box lid.

2 Transfer pocket pattern to green fabric and cut out. Iron fusible web to wrong side of green scraps and star print fabric. (Most pieces will not be fused to box. Applying web adds stability to fabric.) Transfer patterns to fabric and cut 9 trunks from green and 10 trees and 1 trunk from star print.

3 For pocket, fuse ½"-wide strips of fusible web to side and bottom edges on wrong side of pocket. Referring to pattern, turn under side and bottom edges of pocket along fold lines and fuse. Fuse 1 (½"-wide) strip of fusible web to top edge on wrong side of pocket. Turn under top edge of pocket and fuse. Center and fuse 1 tree and star print trunk on right side of pocket.

4 Referring to photo, center and glue side and bottom edges of pocket on box lid. Glue remaining trees and trunks around side of box, spacing evenly. Glue 1 star sequin in place at top of each tree. Let dry. Embellish painted squares and fabric appliqués with dimensional paint as desired. Let dry.

2 Turn under ½" along 1 long edge of 6" x 18" fabric piece and glue, using Tacky Glue. Spread Tacky Glue on outside of carton, leaving ½" at bottom uncovered. With hemmed edge ½" above bottom of carton, cover carton with fabric, leaving excess at top. Overlap ends of fabric, turn top end under ½", and glue, using Tacky Glue. Fold excess fabric at top of carton to inside and glue, using Tacky Glue. Let dry.

3 Glue 1 length of gold braid around bottom of carton, using Designer Tacky Glue. Glue remaining length of gold braid around rim of carton lid, using Designer Tacky Glue. Let dry.

4 Referring to photo and using Designer Tacky Glue, glue ribbon around carton in a zigzag pattern to create drum design. Glue 1 star sequin in place at each ribbon point. Let dry.

5 Cut each long edge of 1½" x 18" fabric strip with pinking shears. Tie fabric strip in bow. Using Designer Tacky Glue, glue fabric bow, assorted trims, and remaining star sequins to box lid as desired (see photo). Let dry. Apply glitter spray to box lid and let dry.

Drum Box

Materials

Oatmeal carton with lid
Gold spray paint
Red-green-and-gold striped fabric: 1 (6" x 18") piece, 1 (1½" x 18") strip
Aleene's Tacky Glue™
2 (19") lengths ½"-wide gold braid
Aleene's Designer Tacky Glue™
33" length ⅛"-wide gold-and-silver ribbon
16 gold metallic star sequins
Pinking shears
Assorted trims: greenery, berries, flowers, cinnamon sticks, star anise
Glitter spray

Directions

1 Draw line around oatmeal carton, 4" from bottom. Cut off top part of carton at marked line and set aside for another use. Spray-paint outside of carton and lid gold. Let dry.

Glue fabric trees to a purchased box for this food gift wrap. Tuck a copy of the recipe into the pocket on the lid.

Turn an empty oatmeal carton into a fancy gift box with some fabric and trims.

Wrap a loaf of bread in holiday print fabric and craft a gift tag and a recipe card, using brown bag gingerbread figures.

Bread Wrap

You can wrap a gift loaf of bread quickly by using a piece of fabric and some ribbon. Just wrap the bread with the fabric as if you were wrapping a gift box and use coordinating ribbon to secure the fabric.

To make the decorated gift tag and the recipe card shown here, transfer the patterns on page 96 and cut 2 each of man and woman gingerbread figures from brown grocery bag and 1 each from lightweight cardboard. To assemble the gingerbread man, squeegee 1 side of 1 cardboard man with Aleene's Tacky Glue™. With the edges aligned, press 1 brown bag man into the glue. Repeat to apply the remaining brown bag man to

the other side of the cardboard. Let dry. In the same manner, assemble the gingerbread woman.

Referring to the photo and using white, bronze metallic, and red dimensional paints, add details to each figure. Let dry. Write the recipe on an index card and glue the gingerbread woman in place. Write the gift tag information on another index card and glue the gingerbread man in place. Let dry. Slip the cards under the ribbon on the wrapped bread.

Creative Wraps

Is there any way to disguise a gift as recognizable as a tennis racket or a compact disc? Just be creative!

Use cardboard cake rounds and tissue paper to turn a tennis racket into a snowman. Try this creative wrap with other items, like a frying pan, a musical instrument, or even a baseball bat.

Snowman Wrap

Materials
Patterns on page 96 and 97
Tennis racket
Cardboard cake rounds: 2 (12"-diameter),
    2 (16"-diameter)
Transparent tape
8 sheets white tissue paper
Fun Foam: orange, black, red
1 sheet black construction paper
Aleene's Stick Glue™
Christmas print fabric: 1 (5¼" x 36") strip,
    1 (2½" x 7¼") strip
Pinking shears

Directions

1 For snowman's head, place 1 (12") cake round on each side of tennis racket head and tape cardboard together at edges, without squeezing edges together. In same manner, place 1 (16") cake round on each side of tennis racket handle and tape cardboard edges together for snowman's body. Tape head and body together. Using 4 sheets of tissue paper each for head and body, wrap cake rounds with tissue paper to cover, securing paper with tape.

2 Transfer patterns and cut 1 nose from orange foam, 1 smile from black foam, and 1 hat from black construction paper. From remaining black foam, cut 5 (1¾"-diameter) circles for eyes and body details. Cut 2 (2¼"-diameter) circles from red foam for cheeks. Referring to photo, glue foam pieces in place on snowman.

3 Trim fabric edges with pinking shears. Knot 5¼" x 36" fabric strip around snowman's neck. Glue 2½" x 7¼" fabric strip to hat for trim, turning ½" at each end of fabric to back. Glue hat to snowman's head.

Compact Disc Pyramid

Materials

Pyramid Diagram on page 98
1 (18") square each lightweight cardboard and
    fabric
Craft knife
Aleene's Fusible Web™
Aleene's Designer Tacky Glue™
7" length ¼"-wide gold braid
1 yard 1"-wide organdy ribbon to match fabric
6" length 26-gauge florist's wire

Directions

Hint: Cereal box cardboard works well for this
project, but be sure printing on box will not show
through fabric.

1 Referring to Pyramid Diagram, measure compact disc and draw pattern on cardboard. (A
standard CD measures 5⅝" wide, 4⅞" high, and
½" deep.) Cut out cardboard piece and score along
all lines as indicated on Pyramid Diagram.

2 Iron fusible web to wrong side of fabric. Place
cardboard piece right side down on paper side
of web and trace. Cut out shape, just outside
marked lines. Center and fuse fabric on right side
of cardboard piece.

3 Put compact disc inside base of pyramid. Fold
pyramid along all score lines. Spread glue on
1 tab and press adjacent tab into glue. Pin tabs
together until glue is dry. Repeat to glue all tabs
together. For hanger, fold gold braid in half and
glue ends inside top of pyramid. Referring to
pages 142 and 143, make multilooped bow with
ribbon and florist's wire. Use tails of wire to attach
bow to hanger.

Gift Baskets

Heidi selected four containers to decorate as gift baskets. Once you've decided on the theme for your gift, check discount stores for an interesting container.

Desk Organizer

For this presentation of office supplies, Heidi decorated a divided basket with the napkin appliqué technique. She suggests filling the basket with pens, pencils, paper clips, stamps, and other handy items for a student away from home.

To do napkin appliqué, you will need a basket, print paper napkins, Aleene's Napkin Appliqué™ Glue, a ½" shader paintbrush, and clear spray sealer. (*Hint:* You may wish to spray-paint the basket white since the color of the basket will show through the napkins.)

To prepare the napkins, cut allover print napkins into small pieces or cut individual motifs from the napkins. Remove bottom plies of napkin to leave the cutouts 1-ply thick. Working over a small area at a time, brush a coat of glue on the basket in the desired position. Press 1 napkin piece into the glue-covered area. Gently brush a coat of glue on top of the napkin piece. Continue until the basket is completely covered, slightly overlapping the napkin pieces for better coverage. Let dry. Coat the basket with spray sealer.

Decoupaged Watering Can

Dress up a watering can and fill it with seed packages and hand tools as a present for a gardener. For a flower-lover, arrange cut or potted flowers in the can with a few seed packages for the garden. To create this container, you will need empty seed packages, garden motif gift wrap cutouts, a metal watering can, Aleene's Instant Decoupage Glue™, a sponge paintbrush, and raffia.

Cut out the desired portion of each seed package. Brush a coat of glue on the watering can in the desired position. Press 1 seed package or gift wrap cutout into the glue-covered area, using your fingers to press out any air bubbles. Brush a coat of glue on top of the cutout, covering the edges of the paper.

Continue to apply the cutouts to the watering can until you get the desired effect. Let dry. Brush a second coat of glue on top of the cutouts. Let dry. Tie the raffia in a bow around the handle of the watering can.

Wine Gift Set

Materials (for basket and 1 glass)

Patterns on page 99
Aleene's Opake Shrink-It™ Plastic
Fine-grade sandpaper
Fine-tip permanent black marker
1/8"-diameter hole punch
Colored pencils: green, yellow, brown
Aleene's Baking Board or nonstick cookie sheet,
   sprinkled with baby powder
Clear spray sealer
Spray paint: gold metallic, red
Wine bottle basket
Aleene's Designer Tacky Glue™
Multicolored novelty yarn (See note below.)
Gold metallic thread
1"-wide red organdy ribbon: 1 (25") length, 1
   (11") length
Wine glass

Directions

Note: Novelty yarns like one pictured here are available in shops that cater to knitters.

1 Sand 1 side of Shrink-It so that markings will adhere. Be sure to thoroughly sand both vertically and horizontally. Using black marker, trace patterns for 6 stars and 4 trees on sanded side of Shrink-It. (Marker ink may run on sanded surface; runs will shrink and disappear during baking.) Cut out each design and punch hole where indicated on pattern. Use colored pencils to color each tree. (Remember that colors will be more intense after shrinking.) Do not color stars. Place designs on baking board and bake in oven as described on page 141.

2 Apply 1 coat of sealer to each tree. Let dry. Spray-paint both sides of each star gold. Let dry. Spray-paint basket red. Let dry. Referring to photo, wrap and glue yarn around top of basket.

3 Measure around basket and add 3". Cut 1 length of metallic thread to that measurement. String 3 trees and 3 stars alternately on metallic thread length, knotting thread to space designs about 1" apart. Tie thread around basket on top of yarn. Cut 1 (15") length each of yarn and metallic thread and tie around basket handle at top. On 1

thread streamer, string 1 star and 1 tree, knotting thread to secure designs. In same manner, attach 1 star to remaining thread streamer. Cut 9 (3") lengths of metallic thread. Tie each thread length in bow and glue 1 bow at top of each design. Let dry. Tie 25" ribbon in bow around basket handle at top. Glue ribbon streamers to handle as desired (see photo).

4 To decorate glass, tie 11" ribbon in bow around glass stem. Wrap yarn several times around stem above bow. Push bow and yarn up to bottom of glass bowl. Cut 1 (8") length of metallic thread. String 1 star on thread, knotting thread to secure design. Tie thread around glass on top of yarn. Cut 1 (3") length of metallic thread. Tie thread in bow and glue in place at top of star. Let dry.

Leafy Planter

Materials

Patterns on page 98
Round wire planter
Basket to fit inside wire planter
Fabric (See Step 1 for amount needed.)
Aleene's No-Sew Fabric Glue™ or thread to
   match fabric and needle
Fine-tip permanent black marker
Waxed paper
Aleene's Fabric Stiffener™
3" square cardboard squeegee
Brown grocery bags
Aleene's Tacky Glue™
8 (6") lengths 22-gauge florist's wire
Acrylic paints: blue-green, white
Small sponge piece
Gold paste paint

Directions

1 Measure interior of planter from 1 top edge, down side, across bottom, and back up to opposite top edge. Add 1" to this measurement. Cut circle of fabric to this measurement. Squeeze line of No-Sew Glue on wrong side of fabric circle around edge. Turn under ¼" around edge and press into glue for hem. Let dry. (*Note:* If desired, stitch ¼" hem around edge of fabric circle.)

2 Using black marker, mark center on right side of fabric with small dot. Cover work surface with waxed paper. With right side up, lay fabric circle on waxed paper and squeegee with fabric stiffener. Turn fabric circle to wrong side and squeegee with fabric stiffener. Place basket in center of fabric. Gather fabric around basket, checking to be sure marked dot is centered on bottom of basket. Place fabric and basket inside planter. Wash and dry hands to remove stiffener. Referring to photo, arrange fabric gathers as desired. Let dry.

3 For leaves, cut 2 (9") squares of brown bag. Transfer patterns for 2 small leaves, 3 medium leaves, and 3 large leaves to 1 bag square. Lay bag square, pattern side up, on top of remaining bag square. Cut out each piece through both layers, cutting ½" outside marked line. With edges

aligned and using Tacky Glue, glue each pair of matching bag pieces together, sandwiching 1 florist's wire length between layers as indicated on pattern. While glue is still wet, trim excess bag from each piece along marked line; do not cut through wire. Let dry. Shape leaves as desired.

4 Refer to Burnt Brown Bag How-to on page 140 to burn each leaf. Let dry. Sponge-paint each leaf with blue-green and white, letting dry between colors. To add gold highlights to each leaf, rub finger in gold paste paint, wipe off excess paint on paper towel, and gently rub finger over leaf. Continue adding gold until you get desired effect. Let dry.

5 Glue leaves to wire planter as desired. Let dry. For each leaf, twist florist's wire once around wire of planter. Twist excess florist's wire around pencil to coil for tendril. Trim wire to desired length.

Fused Gift Boxes

Turn an empty cardboard box into a festive gift wrap by fusing on holiday print fabric. With this quick technique, you can decorate any size or shape of box.

To create a fused fabric gift box, you will need a cardboard box, Aleene's Fusible Web™, print fabric, and Aleene's Designer Tacky Glue™. Carefully open the box until it lies completely flat. Iron the fusible web to the wrong side of the fabric. (See page 138 for tips on working with fusible web.) Place the flattened box right side down on the paper side of the web and trace. Cut out the shape just outside the marked lines. Center and fuse the fabric on the right side of the box. Refold the box into its original shape and glue the flaps in place, leaving 1 end unglued.

Decorate the box by adding a bow or by gluing on other trims. For the small box pictured here, Heidi made the holly leaf package topper from Fun Foam. To make this topper, transfer the pattern on page 99 to green Fun Foam and cut out 2 leaves. Glue the leaves and 3 (10-mm) red beads to the top of the box. On the large box, Heidi created a beautiful bow and accented it with metallic paper stars (see the pattern on page 99).

Napkin Appliqué Greetings

Napkin appliqué cards are so quick and easy to make that you'll have bunches of greetings in no time. As an alternative to using cookie cutters and solid napkins, cut holiday motifs from printed napkins to make these cards.

Materials (for 1 card or tag)

Card stock or heavyweight paper (cut or folded to desired card size)
Solid paper napkins
Christmas motif cookie cutters
Aleene's Paper Napkin Appliqué™ Glue
Paintbrush
Fine glitter in desired colors
Dimensional paints in desired colors
Metallic star sequins
Pinking shears or decorative-edge scissors
⅛"-diameter hole punch
Gold metallic thread

Directions

1 **For each card or tag,** trace cookie cutter on napkin and cut out. Remove bottom plies of napkin to leave cutouts 1-ply thick.

2 To apply cutouts to card, brush coat of glue on card front in desired position. Press 1 cutout into glue-covered area and press out air bubbles. Gently brush coat of glue on top of cutout. Repeat to apply additional cutouts to card front. If desired, sprinkle glitter onto wet glue. Let dry.

3 *Card variations:* Outline motifs and add details with dimensional paints. Let dry. Glue star sequins to card front. Trim card edges, using pinking shears or decorative-edge scissors. For gift tag, punch hole in 1 top corner of card and attach gold metallic thread hanger.

Torn-Paper Angel

The ragged edges of the torn paper pieces give a folk art appeal to this angel. Use up scraps of paper left from other crafts to make angels in a rainbow of colors.

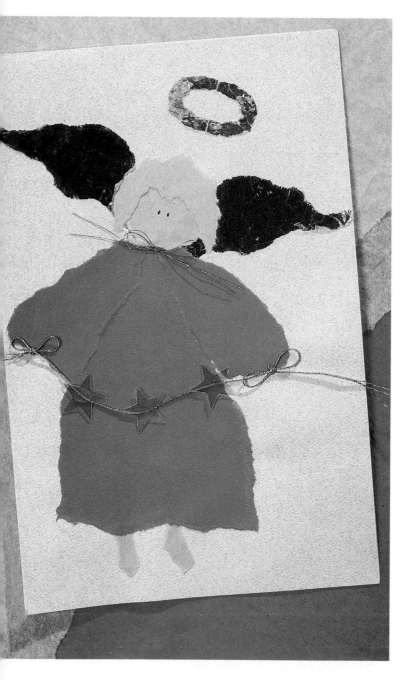

Materials

Patterns on page 99
1 (8½" x 11") piece heavyweight paper
Paper scraps: gold metallic, pink, yellow, turquoise
Aleene's Stick Glue™
Fine-tip permanent black marker
Metallic thread: 2 (6") strands purple, 1 (12")
   length gold
3 iridescent star sequins

Directions

1 Fold heavyweight paper in half widthwise to form card. Referring to photo and patterns, tear paper scraps as follows: 1 halo and 2 wings from gold metallic; 1 face, 2 hands, and 2 feet from pink; 1 hair from yellow; and 1 dress and 2 sleeves from turquoise. Glue paper pieces to card front to form angel (see photo).

2 Draw eyes on face with black marker. Handling both strands of purple thread as 1, tie in bow. Glue bow to angel at neck. Tie a bow at each end of gold thread (see photo). Glue 1 bow to each hand. Referring to photo for placement, glue thread and star sequins to angel.

Button Art

Use buttons and scraps to craft these cute cards. Add a thread hanger to turn a card into a tree ornament.

Materials
For each: Patterns on page 100
1 (4½" x 5½") piece card stock
Aleene's Tacky Glue™
For Santa card: 1 (2" x 2½") piece green-and-tan plaid fabric
Buttons: 1 (½") 2-hole pink, 1 (¾") 2- or 4-hole red
Paper scraps: red, black, gold metallic
Tan fabric scrap
Dimensional paints: black, red, off-white
For snowman card: 1 (2¼" x 2¾") piece red-and-tan plaid fabric
White buttons: 1 (⅜") shank, 1 (⅝") 2-hole
Black paper scrap
Toothpick
Raffia
White sewing thread
Dimensional paints: black, orange, off-white

Directions
1 **For each,** fringe edges of plaid fabric ¼". Center and glue fabric on card stock. Let dry. Referring to photo, center and glue buttons on fabric. Let dry.

2 **For Santa,** transfer patterns and cut the following: 1 hat from red paper and 1 pom-pom, 1 hat trim, 2 mustaches, and 1 beard from tan fabric. Cut 1 (⅛" x ¾") strip of black paper for belt. Cut 1 (¼") square of gold metallic paper for buckle. Fringe curved edge of beard. Glue fabric and paper pieces in place on Santa. Referring to photo and using dimensional paints, draw facial features and arms on Santa. Let dry.

For snowman, transfer snowman hat pattern to black paper and cut out. Glue hat to snowman's head. Let dry. Break off a 1" piece of toothpick for broom handle. Cut 1 (1" x 2") piece of raffia. Fringe 1 long edge of raffia. With fringed edge extending ¾" beyond end of toothpick, wrap raffia around toothpick for broom straw. To secure broom straw to handle, tie thread tightly around bottom edge of raffia and glue in place. Let dry. Referring to photo and using dimensional paints, draw facial features, body details, and arms on snowman. Let dry. Glue broom in place on fabric. Let dry.

Woven Cards

Printed bias tape or ribbon woven through slits cut in card stock form these festive designs. Once you've mastered this technique, you can design your own motifs.

Materials

For each: Patterns on page 100
Foam-core board
Craft knife
Aleene's Tacky Glue™
Fun Foam scrap
1 pencil with eraser
Acrylic paints: green, red
Paintbrush
For ornament card: 1 (6" x 14⅞") piece card stock
18 length ¼"-wide red-and-tan bias tape or ribbon
1⅝" length ¼"-wide gold-and-green braided trim
5" length gold metallic thread
For tree card: 1 (5½" x 13¼") piece card stock, 1 (5⅜" x 6⅛") piece card stock
33" length ¼"-wide green checked bias tape or ribbon

Directions for ornament card

1 Fold card stock in thirds widthwise to form card. Unfold card and tape on foam-core board for work surface. Center and lightly trace ornament pattern on middle panel of card. Using craft knife, gently cut slits in card stock as indicated on pattern.

2 For weaving, cut 6 lengths of bias tape to fit width of pattern. Referring to photo and working from back of middle panel, weave bias tape lengths through strips in card stock, gluing ends at each side of pattern. Let dry. Glue braid to card front for ornament hanger. Tie metallic thread in bow and glue in place at top of ornament. Let dry. With right side facing, fold right-hand panel to back of design and glue. Let dry.

3 **To make star stamp,** transfer star pattern to Fun Foam and cut out. Glue stamp to pencil eraser. Let dry. Referring to photo, paint star stamp with desired color of acrylic paint and press onto card front in desired position. Repeat to paint additional stars on card front. Let dry. To apply a different color of paint to stamp, let paint on stamp dry and then apply new color.

Directions for tree card

1 Fold card stock in half widthwise to form card. Unfold card and tape on foam-core board for work surface. Center and lightly trace tree pattern on card front panel. Using craft knife, gently cut slits in card stock as indicated on pattern.

2 For weaving, cut 9 lengths of bias tape to fit width of pattern. Referring to photo and working from back of card front, weave bias tape lengths through strips in card stock, gluing ends at each side of pattern. Let dry. Referring to Step 3 of ornament card, paint stars on card front as desired. Let dry. Glue remaining card stock to back of card front. Let dry.

Fun Foam Tags

Cut and glue Fun Foam scraps to make these quick tags. Your children will have fun helping you make these.

Materials
Patterns on page 100
Pinking shears
Fun Foam scraps: white, green, red, yellow, black
¼"-diameter hole punch
Aleene's Designer Tacky Glue™
Dimensional paints: black, orange, green
Green embroidery floss scrap
Fine-tip permanent markers: black, red, green

Directions

1 **For each tag,** referring to photo for colors, use pinking shears to cut 1 (1¾" x 2¾") rectangle of Fun Foam.

2 **For poinsettia tag,** transfer patterns to foam scraps and cut 2 green leaves and 8 red petals.

Punch 1 circle from yellow foam scrap. Glue leaves, petals, and circle in place on white tag (see photo). Let dry.

For snowman tag, transfer patterns to foam scraps and cut 1 white head, 1 white body, and 1 black hat. Referring to photo, glue head, body, and hat in place on red tag. Let dry. Using dimensional paints, add details to snowman (see photo). Let dry. Glue green floss to snowman for scarf. Let dry.

For ornaments tag, referring to photo, punch 2 holes in top right corner of green tag. Punch 2 circles from white foam scrap. Glue circles into holes in tag. Let dry. Using markers, draw hanger and design on each ornament (see photo).

Say It with Shrink-It

Deck your gifts with keepsake gift tags. Write the year on the tag and it becomes a treasured ornament for Christmases to come.

Materials (for 3 tags)

Patterns on page 101
Aleene's Opake Shrink-It™ Plastic
Fine-grade sandpaper
Fine-tip permanent black marker
Colored pencils
3/16"-diameter hole punch
Aleene's Baking Board or nonstick cookie sheet, sprinkled with baby powder
Red dimensional paint (optional)
Clear spray sealer
1 (10") length each red and green embroidery floss and gold metallic thread
1 (6") length each red and green embroidery floss (optional)
Aleene's Tacky Glue™

Directions

1 **For each tag,** sand 1 side of Shrink-It so that markings will adhere. Be sure to thoroughly sand both vertically and horizontally. Using black marker, trace pattern on sanded side of Shrink-It. (Marker ink may run on sanded surface; runs will shrink and disappear during baking.) Use colored pencils to color design, coloring white areas first. (Remember that colors will be more intense after shrinking.) Using black marker, add lettering to design. Cut out design and punch hole where indicated on pattern.

2 Place each design on baking board and bake in oven as described on page 141. If desired, add dots of dimensional paint to design. Let dry. Coat design with sealer. Let dry. To attach hanger, fold 1 (10") length of thread in half and knot ends. Thread folded end through hole in design. Thread knotted ends through fold and pull tight to secure. If desired, tie 1 (6") length of embroidery floss in a bow and glue to design. Let dry.

Stained-Glass Box
Directions are on page 63.

Tree

Pretty Plant Pokes
Directions are on page 67.

Butterfly A

Butterfly B

Embellished Glass Ornaments
Directions are on page 69.

Star

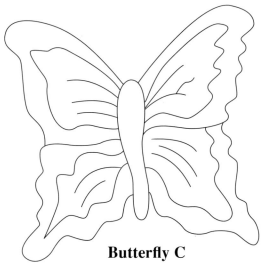

Butterfly C

Holiday Coaster Set
Directions are on page 70.

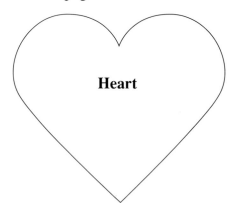

Heart

Star

Stamp-a-Wrap
Directions are on page 74.

Tree

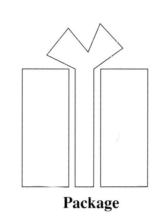

Package

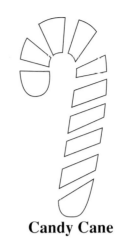

Candy Cane

Star

Gifts of Good Taste:
Trees Box
Directions are on page 77.

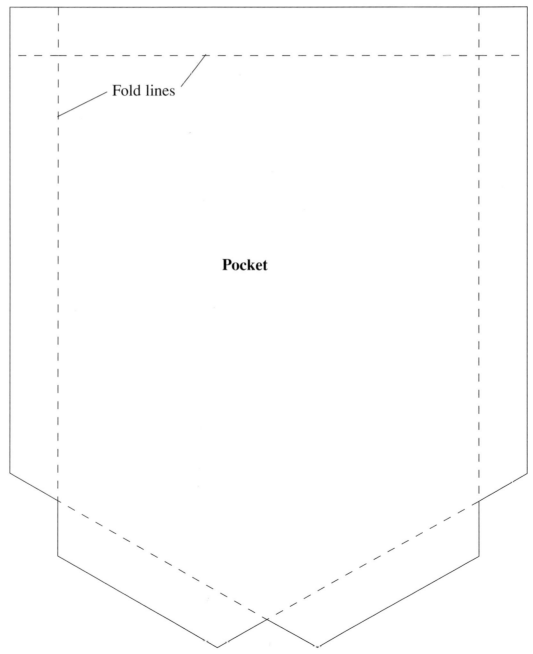

Fold lines

Pocket

Gifts of Good Taste: Trees Box
Directions are on page 77.

Gifts of Good Taste: Bread Wrap
Directions are on page 79.

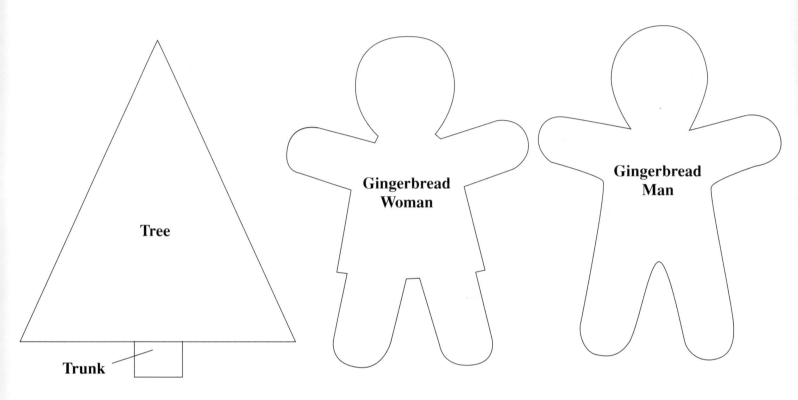

Creative Wraps: Snowman Wrap
Directions are on page 80.

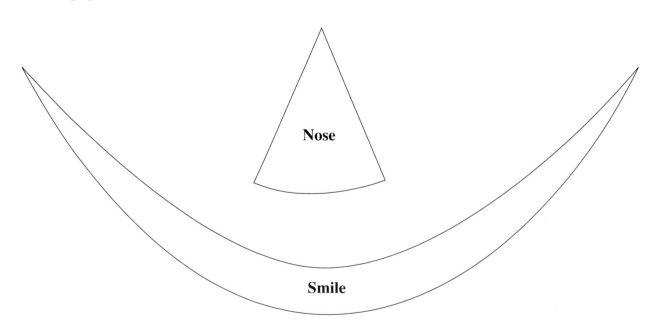

Creative Wraps: Snowman Wrap
Directions are on page 80.

Hat

Place on fold.

Creative Wraps: Compact Disc Pyramid

Directions are on page 81.

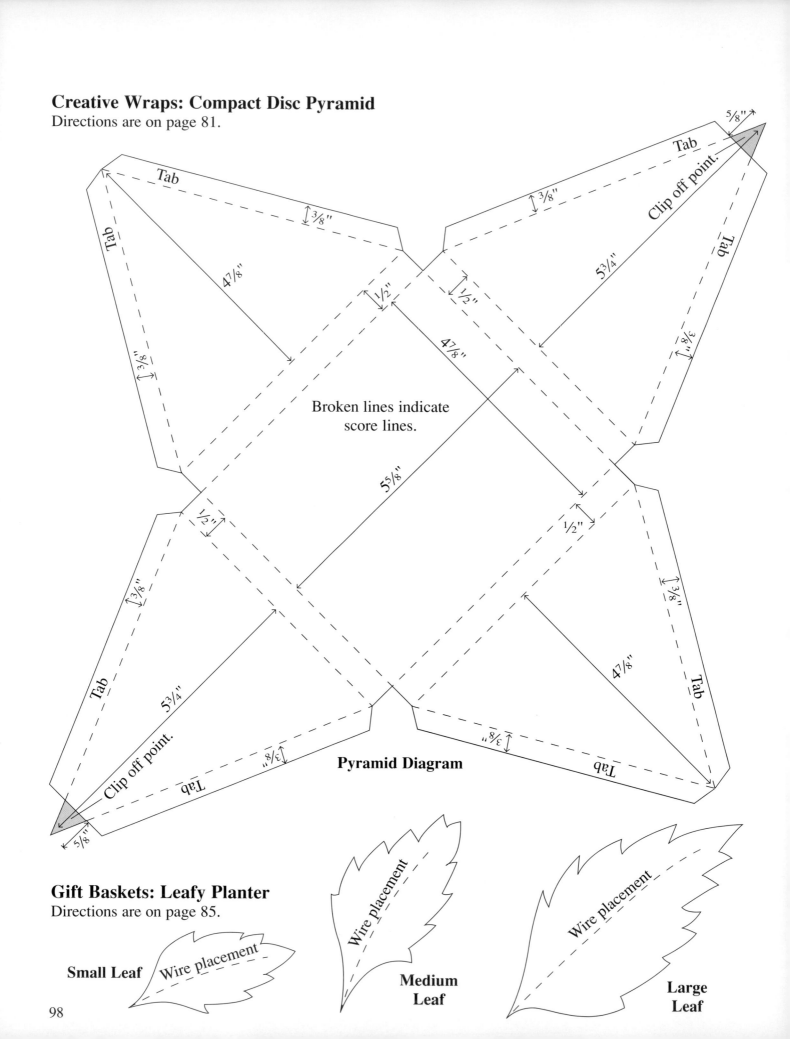

Tab

Tab

5/8"

Tab

Clip off point.

3/8"

3/8"

4⅞"

5¾"

3/8"

1/2"

1/2"

4⅞"

Broken lines indicate score lines.

3/8"

5⅝"

1/2"

3/8"

Tab

5¾"

Clip off point.

Tab

3/8"

Pyramid Diagram

4⅞"

Tab

3/8"

Tab

5/8"

Gift Baskets: Leafy Planter

Directions are on page 85.

Wire placement

Wire placement

Small Leaf

Wire placement

Medium Leaf

Wire placement

Large Leaf

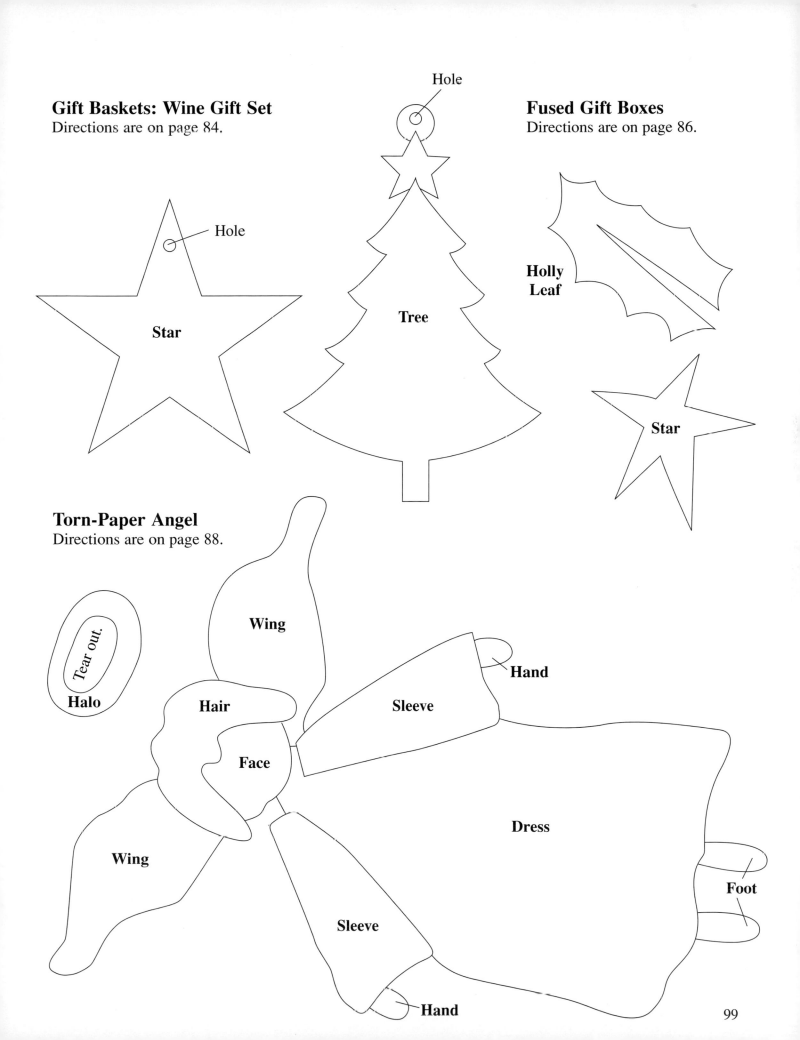

Gift Baskets: Wine Gift Set
Directions are on page 84.

Hole

Star

Hole

Tree

Fused Gift Boxes
Directions are on page 86.

Holly Leaf

Star

Torn-Paper Angel
Directions are on page 88.

Wing

Tear out.

Halo

Hair

Face

Wing

Sleeve

Hand

Dress

Foot

Sleeve

Hand

99

Button Art

Directions are on page 89.

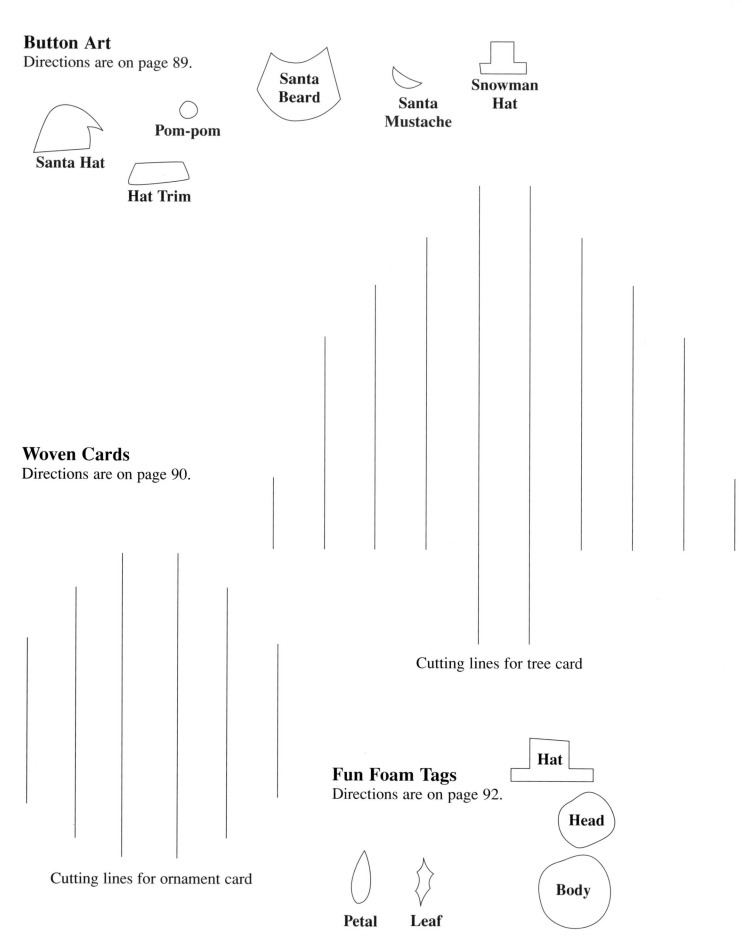

Santa Hat

Pom-pom

Hat Trim

Santa Beard

Santa Mustache

Snowman Hat

Woven Cards

Directions are on page 90.

Cutting lines for tree card

Cutting lines for ornament card

Fun Foam Tags

Directions are on page 92.

Hat

Head

Body

Petal

Leaf

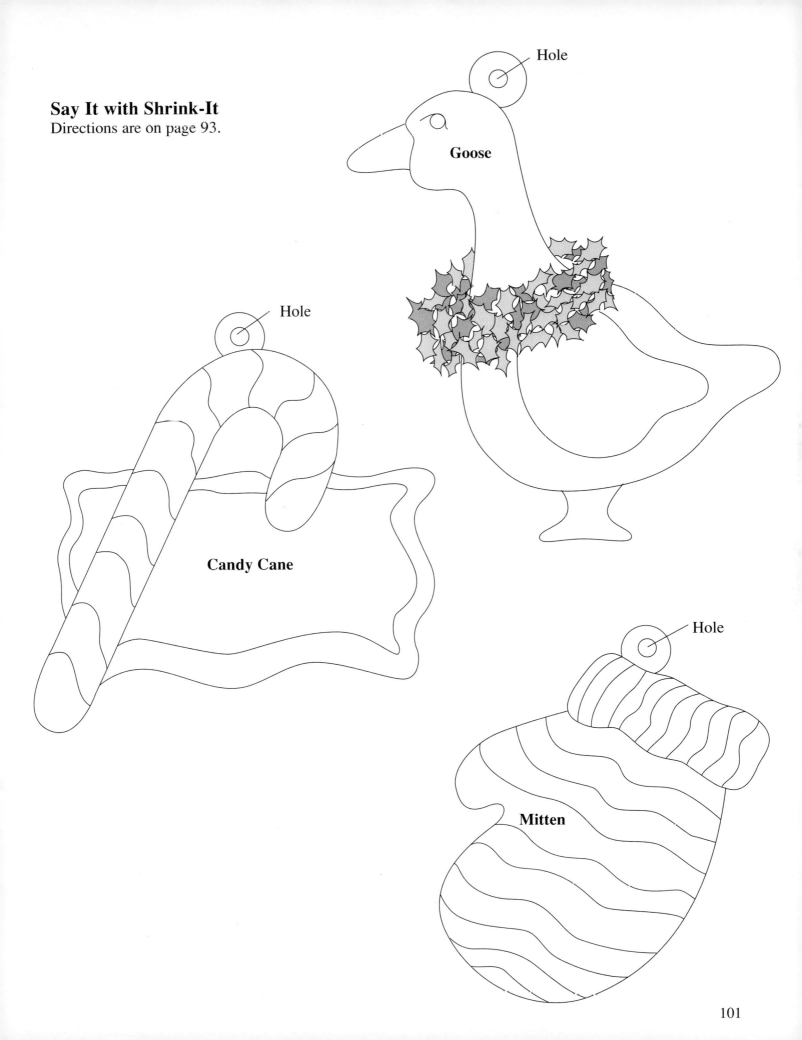

Say It with Shrink-It
Directions are on page 93.

Hole

Goose

Hole

Candy Cane

Hole

Mitten

Festive Fashions

Get ready to be gaily dressed for all sorts of holiday gatherings with this chapter of wearables and jewelry. From a glittering party outfit to a casual napkin-appliqué shirt and jacket, you can create the stylish garments for yourself or for timely gifts.

Glittery Vest &
Colorful Covers

Squeeze lines of glue onto a vest and then sprinkle glitter onto
the glue to create the sparkling motifs shown here. Use the
same patterns to make matching Shrink-It button covers.

Materials

For each: Patterns on pages 130 and 131
For vest: Black vest
Dressmaker's chalk
Cardboard covered with waxed paper
Aleene's OK to Wash-It™ Glue
Glitter: bronze, red, green, white, gold, silver
Aleene's Jewel-It™ Glue
Assorted acrylic jewels
For button covers: Aleene's Opake Shrink-It™
   Plastic
Fine-grade sandpaper
Fine-tip permanent black marker
Colored pencils
Aleene's Baking Board or nonstick cookie sheet,
   sprinkled with baby power
Clear spray sealer
4 metal button covers
2 (14") lengths each ⅛"-wide satin ribbon: red,
   green
4 (2") lengths 22-gauge florist's wire
Aleene's Designer Tacky Glue™

Directions for vest

1 Referring to photo for inspiration and using
  chalk, transfer patterns to vest as desired.
Place cardboard covered with waxed paper inside
vest. Referring to Tape Tip Diagram on page 130,
make tape tip for OK to Wash-It Glue. Working
with 1 pattern and 1 color of glitter at a time,
squeeze line of glue along marked line on vest.
Sprinkle glitter onto wet glue. Let dry. Shake off
excess glitter. Repeat to apply glue and glitter
along remaining marked lines.

2 To adhere each acrylic jewel, squeeze small
  puddle of Jewel-It Glue on vest in desired

position. Press jewel into glue puddle so that glue
comes up around sides of jewel. Let dry.

Directions for button covers

1 **For each,** sand 1 side of Shrink-It so that
  markings will adhere. Be sure to thoroughly
sand both vertically and horizontally. Using black
marker, trace desired pattern on sanded side of
Shrink-It. (Marker ink may run on sanded surface;
runs will shrink and disappear during baking.) Use
colored pencils to color design, coloring white
areas first. (Remember that colors will be more
intense after shrinking.) Cut out design.

2 Place design on baking board and bake in
  oven as described on page 141. Apply 1 coat
of sealer to design.

3 To assemble, sand front of 1 metal button
  cover. Sand back of Shrink-It design. Wrap 1
ribbon length loosely around 3 fingers of 1 hand.
Wrap 1 length of florist's wire securely around
center of ribbon loops. Do not twist wire together
or wrap it too tightly. Pull up and separate ribbon
loops to make flat bow. Glue bow to front of metal
button cover, using Designer Tacky Glue. Glue
Shrink-It design on top of bow, using Designer
Tacky Glue. Let dry.

Embellished Shirt & Jacket

Decorate purchased garments with festive motifs cut from paper napkins. Be sure to completely seal the cutouts with the glue so that your outfit will withstand washing.

Materials

Off-white T-shirt
Off-white sweatshirt jacket
Cardboard covered with waxed paper
Print paper napkins: round Santa, white flowers with leaves and red ribbons (See photo.)
Disappearing-ink pen
Aleene's Paper Napkin Appliqué™ Glue
Paintbrush
Gold glitter dimensional paint
11" length ⅛"-wide red satin ribbon
Aleene's Jewel-It™ Glue
3 tiny jingle bells

Directions

Note: See page 138 for tips on caring for hand-made wearables.

1 Wash and dry shirt and jacket; do not use fabric softener in washer or dryer. Place cardboard covered with waxed paper inside shirt. Referring to photo for inspiration, cut desired motifs from paper napkins. Remove bottom plies of napkin to leave cutouts 1-ply thick.

2 Place Santa napkin cutout on shirt front in desired position. Using disappearing-ink pen, lightly trace around cutout. Remove cutout. Brush coat of Napkin Appliqué Glue on shirt front inside traced line. Place cutout onto glue-covered area and press out any air bubbles. Gently brush top of cutout with coat of Napkin Appliqué Glue. Repeat to apply floral napkin cutouts to shirt as desired (see photo). In same manner, apply floral napkin cutouts to jacket (see photo). Let dry.

3 For shirt and jacket, outline and embellish napkin cutouts with dimensional paint. Let

dry. Tie ribbon in bow. Glue bow to shirt front at neckline, using Jewel-It Glue. Glue bells on top of bow as desired, using Jewel-It Glue. Let dry.

Shoe Trims & Barrette

Dress up plain shoes with a pair of shoe clips made from organdy ribbon and purchased ribbon roses. Create a matching barrette with beads, buttons, and ribbon roses.

Materials

For each: Aleene's Designer Tacky Glue™
For 2 shoe clips: 2 (12") lengths 1"-wide green-and-gold organdy ribbon
Thread to match ribbon and needle
2 (1⅛"-diameter) cardboard circles
2 (20") lengths gold metallic thread
2 red ribbon flowers with leaves
2 shoe clips
For barrette: Barrette with cardboard insert (available in crafts stores)
Fabric scraps: black, small leaf print
Aleene's Fusible Web™
Gold glitter dimensional paint
3 bright red ribbon roses with leaves
Assorted buttons, beads, and pearls

Directions for shoe clips

For each, run gathering thread along 1 long edge of 1 organdy ribbon length. Pull tightly to gather ribbon into circle and secure thread. Center and glue ribbon circle on 1 cardboard circle. Referring to photo, arrange 1 length of gold metallic thread into loops. Glue metallic thread loops to ribbon. Glue 1 ribbon flower on top of metallic thread loops. Let dry. Glue 1 shoe clip to back of cardboard. Let dry.

Directions for barrette

1 Remove insert from barrette. Using insert as guide, cut 1 piece of black fabric ½" larger all around. Center insert on wrong side of black piece. Fold excess fabric to wrong side of insert and glue. Let dry. Replace insert in barrette and glue to secure. Let dry.

2 Iron fusible web to wrong side of leaf print fabric. (*Note:* Leaf print fabric will not be fused. Web is applied to add stability to fabric

cutouts.) Cut desired leaves from fabric. Embellish leaves with dimensional paint. Let dry.

3 Remove paper backing from leaves. Referring to photo, glue leaves, ribbon roses, and assorted buttons, beads, and pearls to barrette. Let dry.

Bread Dough Poinsettia Jewelry

Combine a slice of white bread, a tablespoon of glue, and a dab of paint to make bright poinsettias that look like fine porcelain. These durable flowers make pretty accessories for your Christmas season wearables.

Materials

1 batch red bread dough (See Step 1.)
Yellow seed beads
Aleene's Designer Tacky Glue™
Paintbrush
Cardboard circles: 1 (⅞"-diameter),
  2 (⅝"-diameter)
Red acrylic paint
1 (¾") length thin drinking or cocktail straw
Paper scrap
40" length white satin cording
Plastic beads: 12 (6-mm) green, 6 (8-mm) red
Green florist's tape
2 clip earring backs

Directions

1 Refer to page 139 for bread dough recipe and poinsettia how-to. **For necklace and earrings,** make 1 batch of red bread dough.

   For necklace, make 1 large bread dough poinsettia, using 14 large and 6 small poinsettia petals. Arrange large petals in 2 circular layers with small petals on top (see photo).

   For each earring, make 1 small poinsettia, using 6 large and 6 small poinsettia petals (see photo).

2 For each poinsettia center, pinch off pea-sized ball of red dough. Roll dough into ball. Flatten 1 side of ball. Press in center of petals, with flattened side down. Press seed beads into rounded side of poinsettia center. Let dry. Brush coat of glue on top of seed beads to secure. Let dry.

3 To assemble necklace, paint 1 side of ⅞" cardboard circle red. Let dry. Glue necklace charm poinsettia to painted side of cardboard circle. Let dry. Center and glue straw on back of cardboard circle to make guide for cording. Glue scrap of paper over straw for stability. Let dry. Position poinsettia charm at center of cording. Knot cording on each side of charm. Referring to photo, string beads on each side of charm, knotting cording to secure beads. Glue 1 bead to each end of cording. Let dry.

   To assemble each earring, paint 1 side of ⅝" cardboard circle red. Let dry. Cut 3 (1") lengths of florist's tape. Fold and shape each length of tape to make 1 leaf. Glue 3 leaves to painted side of cardboard circle. Glue 1 earring poinsettia to cardboard on top of leaves (see photo). Let dry. Glue 1 earring back to back of cardboard circle. Let dry.

Easy Holiday Attire

With these patterns, you can decorate a jumper with a sampler of seasonal motifs. Treat your little girl to a dress adorned with a glittering angel.

Materials

For each: Patterns on pages 131 and 132
Aleene's Fusible Web™
Cardboard covered with waxed paper
Assorted colors dimensional paint
For jumper and shirt: Beige-and-green plaid jumper with beige bib
Green T-shirt
Fabric scraps: peach, brown print, red plaid, gold lamé, white, black, green-and-beige plaid, red print
Assorted buttons
Thread to match buttons and needle
For child's dress: Child-sized white knit dress
Fabric scraps: peach, light brown dot, Christmas print, gold lamé
Pop-up craft sponge
Waxed paper
Gold metallic acrylic paint
Aleene's Jewel-It™ Glue
1 (16-mm) yellow plastic star charm

Directions

Note: See page 138 for tips on working with fusible web and on caring for handmade wearables. For jumper, use your favorite pattern to make jumper like 1 shown here or purchase jumper and select appliqué fabrics to match.

1 **For each,** wash and dry garment and fabrics; do not use fabric softener in washer or dryer. Iron fusible web to wrong side of fabrics.

2 **For jumper,** transfer patterns to paper side of web. Cut the following: For angel, cut 2 hands, 2 feet, and 1 (1¼"-diameter) circle for face from peach; 1 hair from brown print; 1 dress and 2 sleeves from red plaid; and 2 wings from gold lamé. For snowman, cut 1 (1⅛"-diameter) circle

for head, 1 (2½"-diameter) circle for body, and 1 arm from white; and 1 hat and 1 boot from black. Reverse patterns and cut another arm from white and another boot from black. For trees, cut 1 whole tree, 1 right half-tree, and 1 left half-tree from green-and-beige plaid. For Santa, cut 1 cap from red print, 1 face from peach, and 1 pom-pom, 1 trim, 1 mustache, and 1 beard from white. Cut 7 stars from gold lamé.

For shirt, transfer pattern to paper side of web and cut 4 whole trees from remaining green-and-beige plaid.

For child's dress, transfer patterns to paper side of web and cut 2 hands, 2 feet, and 1 (1¼"-diameter) circle for face from peach; 1 hair from light brown dot; 1 dress and 2 sleeves from Christmas print; and 2 wings from gold lamé.

3 **For each,** referring to photo for placement, fuse pieces to garment. Place cardboard covered with waxed paper inside garment. Referring to photo, embellish fused appliqués and garment with dimensional paints. Let dry.

For jumper, stitch buttons to jumper bib as desired, using matching thread.

4 **For child's dress,** transfer pattern to sponge and cut 1 star. Place sponge in water to expand and wring out excess water. Pour small puddle of acrylic paint onto waxed paper. Dip sponge into paint and blot excess paint on paper towel. Press sponge onto dress to paint stars as desired (see photo). Let dry. Outline stars with dots of dimensional paint. Let dry. Glue star charm to angel's hands. Let dry.

Tree-Trimmed Shirt

Give an ordinary denim shirt a bold holiday look with fabric scraps and fusible web. Colorful buttons and acrylic paints add the finishing touch.

Materials

Denim shirt
Fabric scraps: brown print, 2 red print star cutouts, 2 different red-and-green plaids, red plaid, 5 different green plaids
Aleene's Fusible Web™
Pinking shears
Aleene's Jewel-It™ Glue
32 assorted buttons for tree ornaments
2 gold heart charms
2 green bow buttons
2 (4") lengths each ⅛"-wide satin ribbon: green, red
Dimensional paints: red, green

Directions

Note: See page 138 for tips on working with fusible web and on caring for handmade wearables.

1 Wash and dry shirt and fabrics; do not use fabric softener in washer or dryer. Iron fusible web to wrong side of fabrics.

2 From brown print, cut 2 (½" x 16") strips. Referring to photo, fuse each strip in place on shirt front for tree trunks. (*Note:* Cut strips apart as needed to leave openings at edge of shirt pockets.) Fuse 1 red print star in place at top of each tree trunk. From red-and-green plaids, cut a total of 2 (1½" x 2½") rectangles and 2 (2¾") squares.

From red plaid, cut 2 (1⅛" x 2½") rectangles. Referring to photo, fuse rectangles and squares in place at bottom of each tree for packages.

3 With pinking shears, cut 16 (1" x 8") strips from green plaid fabrics. Remove paper backing from each strip. Knot center of each strip. Referring to photo, arrange strips on top of each tree trunk for tree branches. Trim ends of strips as needed to shape tree. Fuse strips in place.

4 Referring to photo, glue 1 button to each end of each strip. Glue 1 gold charm to each red star. Glue 1 bow button to each red plaid package. Tie each ribbon length in bow. Glue bows to red-and-green plaid packages as desired. Let dry.

5 To decorate shirt buttons, apply coat of dimensional paint to surface of each button, alternating red and green. Let dry.

Mother-Daughter Outfits

You and your little girl will be dressed in style for the holidays with these coordinated outfits. Simple fabric shapes fused to purchased garments make it easy to adapt these designs to your personal taste or gift-giving needs.

Materials

For each: Patterns on page 132
Fabric dye (See note below.)
Fabric scraps: beige print, green print
Aleene's Fusible Web™
Cardboard covered with waxed paper
Assorted colors dimensional paint
Assorted buttons
Thread to match buttons and needle
For tunic and pants: White knit tunic and pants
Letters guide
Fun Foam scraps
2 pencils with erasers
Aleene's Designer Tacky Glue™
Assorted colors acrylic paint
Waxed paper
For romper: White knit romper
Tiny jingle bells
Gold star button
⅛"-wide satin ribbon: 1 (8") length and 4 (5")
  lengths dark red, 3 (5") lengths navy
Aleene's OK to Wash-It™ Glue

Directions

Note: See page 138 for tips on working with fusible web and on caring for handmade wearables. Heidi used fabric dye to get look of tea-dyed fabric without using tea.

1 For each, wash and dry garments and fabrics; do not use fabric softener in washer or dryer. Following manufacturer's directions, dye garments. Let dry. Iron fusible web to wrong side of fabrics.

2 For tunic, transfer patterns to fabric and cut 7 large hearts from beige print and 8 trees from green print.

For romper, transfer patterns to fabric and cut 1 large heart, 2 medium hearts, 2 small hearts, and 3 tiny hearts from remaining beige print. From remaining green print, cut 1 (5" x 5¾") piece, 2 (3") squares, 1 (2¼" x 4") piece, and 1 (2" x 5") piece. Fringe edges of each green print piece. Center and fuse large heart on 5" x 5¾" piece. Center and fuse 1 medium heart on each 3" square. Fuse small hearts side by side on 2¼" x 4" piece. Fuse tiny hearts in a column on 2" x 5" piece.

3 For each, referring to photo, fuse appliqués to garment. Place cardboard covered with waxed paper inside garment. Embellish fused appliqués with dimensional paints. Let dry.

For tunic, draw wavy lines on tunic with dimensional paints. Let dry. Using letters guide, add lettering to tunic with dimensional paints. Let dry. Transfer patterns to Fun Foam scraps and cut 1 star and 1 stamp heart. Glue 1 foam cutout to each pencil eraser, using Designer Tacky Glue. Let dry. To stamp designs on tunic, pour separate small puddles of acrylic paints onto waxed paper. Dip 1 stamp into 1 paint color and press onto tunic. Repeat as desired. Let dry. To apply different color of paint to stamp, let paint on stamp dry; dip stamp into new color and repeat in same manner as above.

4 For tunic, stitch buttons in place for tree trunks and tree toppers. Referring to photo, stitch additional buttons to tunic as desired.

For romper, stitch assorted buttons and bells to romper as desired. Stitch gold star button to romper at neckline. Tie each ribbon length in bow. Glue bows to appliqués, using OK to Wash-It Glue (see photo). Let dry.

Shimmering Party Outfit

Glittery designs make a plain black dress, black shoes, and a pair of black hose festive enough for a fancy holiday party.

Materials

For jumper and turtleneck: Patterns on page 133
Black knit jumper
Black knit turtleneck
Holly print fabric
Cardboard covered with waxed paper
Freezer paper
Craft knife
1 sheet white paper
Aleene's OK to Wash-It™ Glue
Paintbrush
Glitter: purple, blue, bright pink, gold, red
Aleene's Fusible Web™
3 (4") lengths ⅛"-wide gold metallic ribbon
Aleene's Opake Shrink-It™ Plastic
Fine-grade sandpaper
Fine-tip permanent black marker
Colored pencils
⅛"-diameter hole punch
Aleene's Baking Board or nonstick cookie sheet, sprinkled with baby powder
Clear spray sealer
Gold thread and needle
For panty hose: Pattern on page 133
1 pair black panty hose
Dressmaker's chalk
Cardboard covered with waxed paper
Fun Foam scrap
2" square foam-core board
Aleene's Designer Tacky Glue™
Waxed paper
Acrylic paints: green, red
Pencil with eraser
Dimensional paints: gold glitter, red glitter
For shoes: Fabric scraps: holly print, black
Aleene's Fusible Web™
Aleene's Stop Fraying™ Glue
3" square cardboard squeegee
Aleene's OK to Wash-It™ Glue
Glitter: gold, red

Aleene's Tack-It Over & Over™ Glue
1 pair black shoes

Directions for jumper and turtleneck

Note: See page 138 for tips on working with fusible web and on caring for handmade wearables.

1 Wash and dry jumper, turtleneck, and fabric; do not use fabric softener in washer or dryer. Place cardboard covered with waxed paper inside jumper.

2 For each stencil, cut piece of freezer paper 1" larger all around than ornament pattern. Center pattern and transfer to freezer paper. Cut out and discard ornament. Arrange stencil, wax side down, in desired position on jumper. Place white paper over stencil to protect knit fabric. Press with iron for a few seconds to adhere freezer paper to jumper. Set aside white paper. Brush thin coat of OK to Wash-It Glue on jumper inside stencil. Sprinkle desired color of glitter for ornament onto wet glue, using gold glitter for hanger at top. Let dry. Shake off excess glitter. Remove freezer paper stencil.

3 Iron fusible web to wrong side of holly print. Cut desired motifs from fabric. Arrange holly motifs around neckline of jumper as desired. Place white paper on top of motifs to protect knit fabric. Fuse motifs to jumper. Set aside white paper. In same manner, fuse holly motifs to collar of turtleneck (see photo).

4 Referring to Tape Tip Diagram on page 130, make tape tip for OK to Wash-It Glue. Referring to photo, outline fused motifs and draw veins on leaves and stars on jumper with glue. Sprinkle gold glitter onto wet glue. Let dry. Shake off excess glitter. Add dots of glue to fused motifs for holly berries. Sprinkle red glitter onto wet glue. Let dry. Shake off excess glitter. Repeat to add gold and red glitter to fused motifs on turtleneck. Tie each length of gold metallic ribbon in

bow. Glue 1 bow at top of each ornament, using OK to Wash-It Glue. Let dry.

5 Sand 1 side of Shrink-It so that markings will adhere. Be sure to thoroughly sand both vertically and horizontally. Using black marker, trace small ornaments A and B on sanded side of Shrink-It. (Marker ink may run on sanded surface; runs will shrink and disappear during baking.) Use colored pencils to color each ornament as desired. (Remember that colors will be more intense after shrinking.) Cut out each ornament and punch hole where indicated.

6 Place each ornament on baking board and bake in oven as described on page 141. Apply 1 coat of sealer to each ornament. Stitch ornaments to collar of turtleneck (see photo).

Directions for panty hose

Note: See page 138 for tips on caring for handmade wearbles.

1 Wash hose; do not use fabric softener. Let hose air dry. Put on hose and use dressmaker's chalk to mark desired position of sponge-painted designs on each leg. Take off hose. Place cardboard covered with waxed paper inside 1 leg of hose at a time and center beneath marked area.

2 Transfer pattern to Fun Foam and cut 1 holly leaf. Center and glue foam leaf on foam-core board. Pour separate puddles of red and green paint onto waxed paper. Dip leaf stamp into green paint and press onto hose within marked area. Repeat until you get desired effect. Dip pencil eraser into red paint and dot on hose for holly berries. Let dry. Outline holly leaves and add details with gold glitter dimensional paint. Outline holly berries with red glitter dimensional paint. Let dry.

Directions for shoes

1 Wash and dry fabrics; do not use fabric softener in washer or dryer. Iron fusible web to wrong side of holly print. With wrong sides facing, fuse print to black fabric. Using cardboard squeegee, apply thin coat of Stop Fraying Glue to black fabric. Let dry.

2 Referring to Tape Tip Diagram on page 130, make tape tip for OK to Wash-It Glue. Referring to photo, outline leaves and draw leaf

Sponge-paint holly leaves on black hose. For perfectly round circles, use a pencil eraser to paint the holly berries. Inexpensive black shoes get dressed up for a night on the town with a little print fabric.

details with glue. Sprinkle gold glitter onto wet glue. Let dry. Shake off excess glitter. Add dots of glue to fabric for holly berries. Sprinkle red glitter onto wet glue. Let dry. Shake off excess glitter. Cut out desired motif for each shoe, cutting close to glitter lines. Apply thin coat of Tack-It Over & Over Glue to back of each motif. Let dry. Press 1 motif onto each shoe.

Poinsettia Print Scarf Set

Fuse motifs cut from pretty holiday print fabric to a scarf and a pair of gloves for a super-quick last-minute gift.

Materials

Scarf (See note below.)
1 pair gloves (See note below.)
Poinsettia print fabric
Aleene's Fusible Web™
1 sheet white paper
Gold glitter dimensional paint

Directions

Note: See page 138 for tips on working with fusible web and on caring for handmade wearables. Use washable scarf and gloves.

1 Wash and dry scarf, gloves, and fabric; do not use fabric softener in washer or dryer. Iron fusible web to wrong side of fabric. Cut desired motifs from fabric.

2 Arrange motifs on scarf. Lay white paper over motifs for pressing cloth and fuse motifs to scarf. Remove paper. In same manner, fuse motifs to each glove.

3 Embellish fused motifs with dimensional paint. Let dry.

Angelic Warmers

Small scraps of fabric and a few dabs of glitter paint are all you need to create these heavenly warmers.

Materials

Patterns on page 133
Scarf (See note below.)
1 pair gloves (See note below.)
Fabric scraps: gold lamé, tan suede, peach cotton
Aleene's Fusible Web™
1 sheet white paper
Fine-tip permanent markers: black, blue, pink
Buttons: 1 (¾") gold heart, 2 (1") white 2-hole,
  2 (⅝") gold hearts
Aleene's Jewel-It™ Glue
Gold glitter dimensional paint
7 (4-mm) gold acrylic jewels
White thread and needle
Off-white yarn scraps
4 (3-mm) black half-round bead eyes

Directions

Note: See page 138 for tips on working with fusible web and on caring for handmade wearables. Use washable scarf and gloves.

1 **For each,** wash and dry scarf, gloves, and fabrics; do not use fabric softener in washer or dryer. Iron fusible web to wrong side of fabrics.

2 **For scarf,** transfer patterns to paper side of web and cut 1 large wings from gold lamé and 1 hair from suede. Cut 1 (2⅝"-diameter) circle from peach cotton for face.

  For each glove, transfer pattern to paper side of web and cut 1 small wings from remaining gold lamé.

3 **For each,** referring to photo, arrange appliqués on garment. Lay white paper over appliqués for pressing cloth and fuse appliqués in place. Remove paper.

4 **For scarf,** referring to photo and *Face Diagram,* draw facial features, using permanent markers. Glue ¾" heart button to scarf below face. Let dry. Draw halo and 7 stars on scarf with dimensional paint (see photo). While paint is still wet, press 1 jewel in center of each star. Let dry.

  For each glove, sitch 1 white button to glove for face (see photo). Stitch yarn scraps to glove for hair. Arrange and glue yarn on white button. Stitch 1 (⅝") heart button to glove below face. Glue 1 bead eye to each buttonhole. Let dry. Draw halo on glove with dimensional paint. Let dry.

Face Diagram

Star Santa Jewelry

Make star-shaped Santas and gift packages with Shrink-It and combine them for a playful set of jewelry to accent a holiday outfit.

Materials

Pattern on page 134
Aleene's Opake Shrink-It™ Plastic
Fine-grade sandpaper
Fine-tip permanent black marker
Colored pencils
⅛"-diameter hole punch
Aleene's Baking Board or nonstick cookie sheet, sprinkled with baby powder
Clear spray sealer
Assorted colors embroidery floss
Aleene's Designer Tacky Glue™
Jewelry findings: 2 (28-mm) ear hoops, 16 (4-mm) jump rings, 2 fishhook earrings, 20" necklace chain, necklace clasp
Needlenose pliers

Directions

1 Sand 1 side of Shrink-It so that markings will adhere. Be sure to thoroughly sand both vertically and horizontally. Using black marker, trace Santa pattern 3 times on sanded side of Shrink-It. Using black marker, draw 6 (1" x 1¼") rectangles on sanded side of Shrink-It for packages. (Marker ink may run on sanded surface; runs will shrink and disappear during baking.) Use colored pencils to color each design, coloring white areas first. (Remember that colors will be more intense after shrinking.) Cut out each design. For 1 Santa, punch 1 hole in each hand. For remaining Santas, punch 2 holes in hat tip, just below hat pom-pom. For each package, punch 1 hole in each of 2 opposite corners (see photo).

2 Place each design on baking board and bake in oven as described on page 141. Apply 1 coat of sealer to each design. For each package, tie embroidery floss in bow and glue to package. Let dry.

3 To assemble each earring, use embroidery floss to stitch 1 Santa with holes in hat to 1 ear hoop. Using pliers and 1 jump ring, attach ear hoop to fishhook earring. To assemble necklace, attach 1 jump ring to each hole in each design, using pliers. Referring to photo, divide necklace chain into several short lengths. Attach jump rings in designs to lengths of chain to form necklace. Attach clasp to ends of chain.

Snowman Dress

Stitch a fabric skirt to a knit T-shirt to make this sweet little dress. Embellish the dress with fused and painted designs.

Materials

Patterns on page 134
T-shirt
Print fabric to match T-shirt for skirt (See Step 1.)
Thread to match fabric and needle
Fabric scraps: white-on-white print, black
Aleene's Fusible Web™
Cardboard covered with waxed paper
Pop-up craft sponges
Acrylic paints: white, green
Waxed paper
Assorted colors dimensional paint
5" lengths ¼"-wide satin ribbon: 3 red, 1 green
Aleene's OK to Wash-It™ Glue

Directions

Note: See page 138 for tips on working with fusible web and on caring for handmade wearables.

1 Wash and dry shirt and fabrics; do not use fabric softener in washer or dryer. Measure around bottom of T-shirt. Multiply this measurement by 2½. Put shirt on child and measure from bottom of shirt to determine desired length of skirt. Add 1" to this measurement. Cut print fabric to these measurements for skirt.

2 Turn under ¼" twice along 1 long edge of fabric and stitch for hem. Run 2 gathering threads along remaining long edge of fabric. With right sides facing and raw edges aligned, stitch short ends of fabric together to form a tube. Pull threads to gather skirt to fit bottom of shirt. With right sides facing and gathered edge aligned with hemmed edge of shirt, stitch skirt to shirt.

3 Iron fusible web to wrong side of white and black fabrics. Cut 3 (1¼"-diameter) circles and 3 (2¼"-diameter) circles from white. Transfer patterns to paper side of web and cut 3 hats and 3 boots from black. Fuse appliqués to dress.

4 Place cardboard covered with waxed paper inside dress. Transfer pattern to sponge and cut 1 tree. From remaining sponge, cut 1 (¾" x ⅞")

rectangle. Place each sponge in water to expand and wring out excess water. Pour separate small puddles of white and green paint onto waxed paper. Dip tree sponge into green paint and blot excess paint on paper towel. Press sponge onto dress. Repeat as desired (see photo). In same manner, paint white rectangles on dress (see photo). Let dry. Embellish fused appliqués and sponge-painted designs and paint snowflakes on dress with dimensional paints (see photo). Let dry.

5 Tie each ribbon length in bow. Referring to photo, glue 2 red bows and 1 green bow to snowmen. Glue remaining red bow to front of dress at neckline. Let dry.

Holly Jolly Outfit

Here's an outfit to keep your child warm on cold December days. A paper napkin heart framed in pretty lace adorns the shirt, and bright buttons and bows complete the design.

Materials)

Child-sized beige shirt and pants
Cardboard covered with waxed paper
1 (4¾" x 7") lace frame appliqué with heart-shaped opening
Holly print napkin
Disappearing-ink pen
Aleene's Paper Napkin Appliqué™ Glue
Paintbrush
Aleene's OK to Wash-It™ Glue
⅛"-wide satin ribbon: 30" length red, 24" length green
Aleene's Jewel-It™ Glue
Buttons: 2 green stars, 9 green-and-red flowers, 2 green leaves

Directions

Note: See page 138 for tips on caring for handmade wearables.

1 Wash and dry shirt and pants; do not use fabric softener in washer or dryer. Place cardboard covered with waxed paper inside shirt.

2 Trace heart opening in lace appliqué onto wrong side of napkin. Cut out heart. Remove bottom plies of napkin to leave cutout 1-ply thick. Place napkin heart on shirt front. Lightly trace around heart with disappearing-ink pen. Remove cutout. Brush coat of Napkin Appliqué Glue on shirt front inside traced line. Place cutout onto glue-covered area and press out any air bubbles. Gently brush top of cutout with coat of Napkin Appliqué Glue. Let dry.

3 Brush coat of OK to Wash-It Glue on back of lace appliqué. With appliqué opening aligned with napkin heart, glue appliqué on shirt front. Let dry.

4 From ribbons, cut 6 (4") lengths of red and 6 (4") lengths of green. Tie each ribbon length in bow. (*Note:* Use Jewel-It Glue to adhere bows and buttons to outfit.) Glue 1 red bow on front of each pant leg, just above cuff. Roll up each sleeve 2 or 3 times. Glue 1 green bow on front of each rolled sleeve cuff. Glue remaining bows on shirt front as desired. Let dry. Glue 1 star button on top of each bow on pants. Glue 1 flower button on top of each of 8 bows on shirt front. Let dry.

5 Tie remaining red ribbon in bow. Center and glue bow at top of lace appliqué. Let dry. Glue 1 leaf button to lace appliqué on each side of bow. Glue remaining flower button on top of bow. Let dry.

Dino-Shirt

Fuse a dinosaur with a Christmas-print wreath around its neck to a plain sweatshirt to make playclothes for a boy or a girl. Create the border design with fused fabric squares and dots of dimensional paint.

Materials

Patterns on page 134
Green sweatshirt
Fabric scraps: red-and-green plaid, holly print
Aleene's Fusible Web™
Pinking shears
Cardboard covered with waxed paper
Dimensional paints: green, black, red
6" length ⅜"-wide white polka dot ribbon
Aleene's OK to Wash-It™ Glue

Directions

Note: See page 138 for tips on working with fusible web and on caring for handmade wearables.

1 Wash and dry shirt and fabrics; do not use fabric softener in washer or dryer. Iron fusible web to wrong side of fabrics. Transfer patterns to paper side of web and cut 1 dinosaur, 1 partial back leg, and 1 partial front leg from plaid. Transfer pattern to paper side of web and cut 1 wreath from holly print, using pinking shears. From remaining holly print, cut 9 (1⅛") squares.

2 Referring to photo, fuse appliqués to shirt front. Place cardboard covered with waxed paper inside shirt. Embellish fused appliqués with dimensional paint. Let dry. Tie ribbon in bow and glue to wreath. Let dry.

Sponge-Painted Bibs

Dress your baby for Christmas dinner with a quick-and-easy bib. Simply add a sponge-painted design to a purchased bib and glue on lace and rickrack.

Materials

Patterns on page 135
2 white baby bibs
Pop-up craft sponges
Waxed paper
Acrylic paints: red, green, gold, pink
Dimensional paints: gold, green, black
Aleene's OK to Wash-It™ Glue
1 gold star button
1 length each white lace and rickrack for each bib
  (See photo and Step 3.)

Directions

Note: See page 138 for tips on caring for hand-made wearables.

1 **For each,** wash and dry bibs; do not use fabric softener in washer or dryer. Transfer patterns to sponges and cut 1 each. Place each sponge in water to expand and wring out excess water. Pour separate small puddles of acrylic paints onto waxed paper.

2 **For angel bib,** dip dress sponge into red paint and blot excess paint on paper towel. Press sponge onto bib in desired position. In same manner, paint angel's head, sleeve, wing, hand, and feet on bib (see photo for colors). Let dry. Referring to photo, paint details with dimensional paints. Let dry. Glue button to angel's hand. Let dry.

  For stocking bib, paint stocking and details as for angel bib.

3 **For each,** measure around edge of bib from 1 side of neck opening, around bottom of bib, and up to other side of neck opening. Add ½" to this measurement. Cut 1 length each of lace and rickrack to this measurement. Squeeze line of glue around edge on right side of bib from 1 side of neck opening, around bottom of bib, and up to other side of neck opening. Press bound edge of

lace into glue so that lace extends beyond edge of bib. Turn under ¼" at each end of lace and glue. Squeeze line of glue around edge of bib on top of bound edge of lace. Press rickrack into glue, covering edge of lace. Turn under ¼" at each end or rickrack and glue. Let dry.

Wearables Kids Can Make

Let your children prepare for the holidays by adding glitter designs to a pair of shoes or by gluing buttons on a hat and mittens. For Christmas Eve sleepwear, your little ones can block-print a reindeer on a large T-shirt.

Decorated Shoes

Materials

For each: Patterns on page 135
1 pair white sneakers
Fun Foam scraps
1 pencil with eraser
Aleene's Designer Tacky Glue™
Waxed paper
Aleene's OK to Wash-It™ Glue
Paintbrush
For star shoes: Gold acrylic paint
Toothpick
Gold glitter
Pony beads: 6 gold, 4 gold sparkle
For holly shoes: Acrylic paints: green, red
1" x 2" piece foam-core board
Iridescent glitter
4 green pony beads
2 red plastic Santa beads

Directions

Note: See page 138 for tips on caring for hand-made wearables.

1 **For each,** remove shoelaces from shoes. Wash shoes; do not use fabric softener in washer. Let shoes air dry. Stuff wads of clean paper or fabric inside shoes to provide firm surface for decorating.

2 **For star shoes,** transfer pattern to Fun Foam and cut 1 star. Glue star to 1 pencil eraser, using Designer Tacky Glue. Let dry. Pour puddle of gold paint onto waxed paper. Dip foam star into paint and press onto shoes. Repeat until you get desired effect. Dip 1 end of toothpick into paint and paint dots on shoes as desired. Let dry.

For holly shoes, transfer pattern to Fun Foam and cut 1 holly leaf. Glue holly leaf to foam-core board, using Designer Tacky Glue. Let dry. Pour separate puddles of green and red paint onto waxed paper. Dip foam holly leaf into green paint and press onto shoes. Dip pencil eraser into red paint and press onto shoes to paint holly berries. Repeat until you get desired effect. Let dry.

3 **For each,** brush coat of OK to Wash-It Glue over painted design. Sprinkle glitter onto wet glue. Let dry. Shake off excess glitter. Referring to photo, thread beads on each lace and put laces in shoes.

Button Trees Hat & Mittens

Materials

Knit hat
1 pair knit mittens
Cardboard covered with waxed paper
Aleene's Jewel-It™ Glue
Assorted buttons: 21 green, 3 red, 3 gold star

Directions

Note: See page 138 for tips on caring for hand-made wearables.

1 For each, wash and dry hat and mitens; do not use fabric softener in washer or dyer. To glue each button in place, squeeze small puddle of glue in desired position. Press button into glue puddle so that glue comes up around sides and through holes in button.

2 For hat, place cardboard covered with waxed paper inside hat. Referring to photo, glue 9 green buttons on hat to form tree. Glue 1 red button to hat at bottom of tree for trunk. Glue 1 star button at top of tree. Let dry.

For each mitten, place cardboard covered with waxed paper inside mitten. Referring to photo, glue 6 green buttons on mitten to form tree. Glue 1 red button at bottom of tree for trunk. Glue 1 star button at top of tree. Let dry.

Reindeer Sleep Shirt

Materials

Pattern on page 135
Large red T-shirt
Cardboard covered with waxed paper
Fun Foam scraps
3¼" x 5½" piece foam-core board
Aleene's Designer Tacky Glue™
Brown acrylic paint
Paintbrush
Dimensional paints: black, gold glitter
Letters guide or ruler
1 (¾"-diameter) red pom-pom
Aleene's OK to Wash-It™ Glue
6" length ¼"-wide green ribbon

Directions

Note: See page 138 for tips on caring for hand-made wearables.

1 Wash and dry shirt; do not use fabric softener in washer or dryer. Place cardboard covered with waxed paper inside shirt. Transfer pattern to Fun Foam and cut 1 reindeer head. Using Designer Tacky Glue, center and glue foam cutouts on foam-core board, leaving space between pieces as indicated on pattern. Let dry.

2 Paint foam reindeer brown. Position reindeer on shirt and press firmly, being sure all areas of stamp come into contact with shirt. Carefully lift stamp off shirt. Let dry.

3 Referring to photo, draw eyes and antlers on reindeer with dimensional paints. Using letters guide, add lettering to shirt with gold dimensional paint. Let dry. Glue pom-pom nose to reindeer head, using OK to Wash-It Glue. Tie ribbon in bow and glue to bottom of reindeer head, using OK to Wash-It Glue. Let dry.

Tape Tip Diagram

Refer to Glittering Glue Snowflakes on page 24, Glittery Vest &
Colorful Covers on page 105, and Shimmering Party Outfit on page 117.

1. Using 4"-long piece of transparent tape, align 1 long edge of tape with edge of nozzle as shown. Press tape firmly to nozzle to prevent leaks.

2. Rotate bottle to wrap tape around tip.

3. Continue rotating bottle and wrapping tape until tape reverses direction and winds back down toward bottle.

4. Press tail of tape to bottle for easy removal.

Glittery Vest & Colorful Covers

Directions are on page 105.

Glittery Vest &
Colorful Covers
Directions are on page 105.

Easy Holiday Attire
Directions are on page 111.

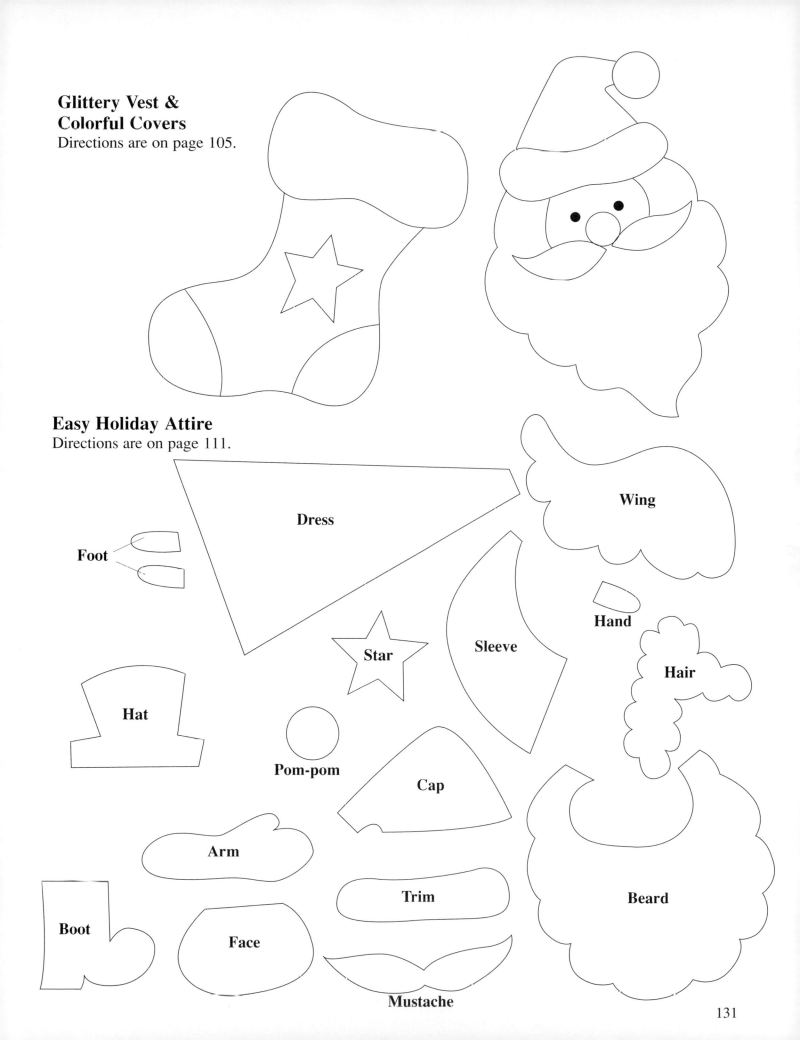

Foot

Dress

Wing

Hand

Star

Sleeve

Hair

Hat

Pom-pom

Cap

Arm

Trim

Beard

Boot

Face

Mustache

Easy Holiday Attire
Directions are on page 111.

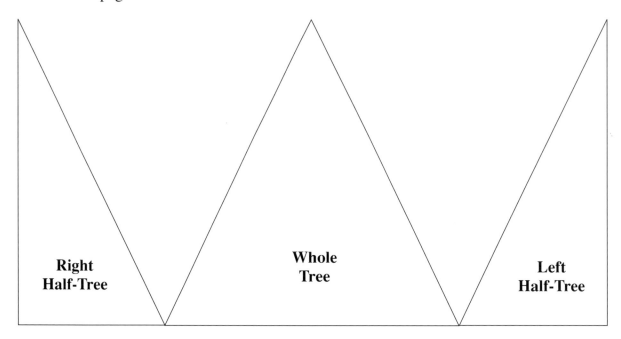

Right Half-Tree

Whole Tree

Left Half-Tree

Mother-Daughter Outfits
Directions are on page 115.

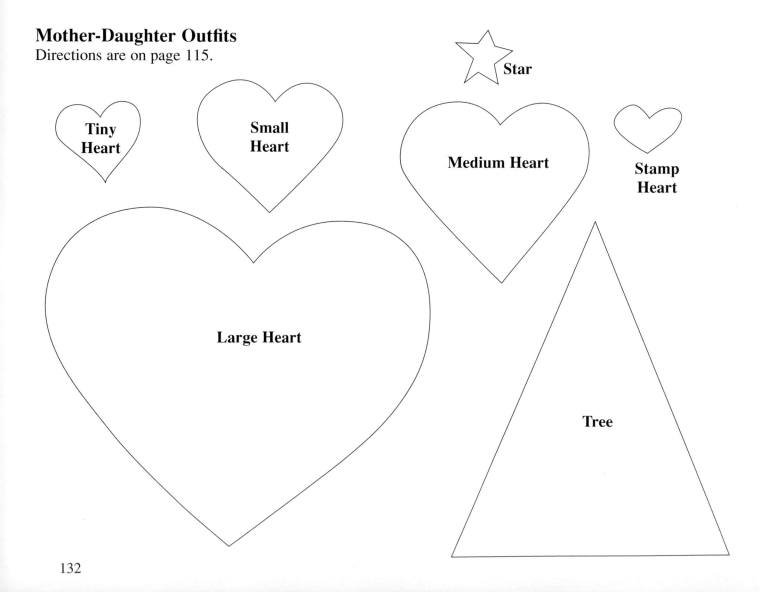

Star

Tiny Heart

Small Heart

Medium Heart

Stamp Heart

Large Heart

Tree

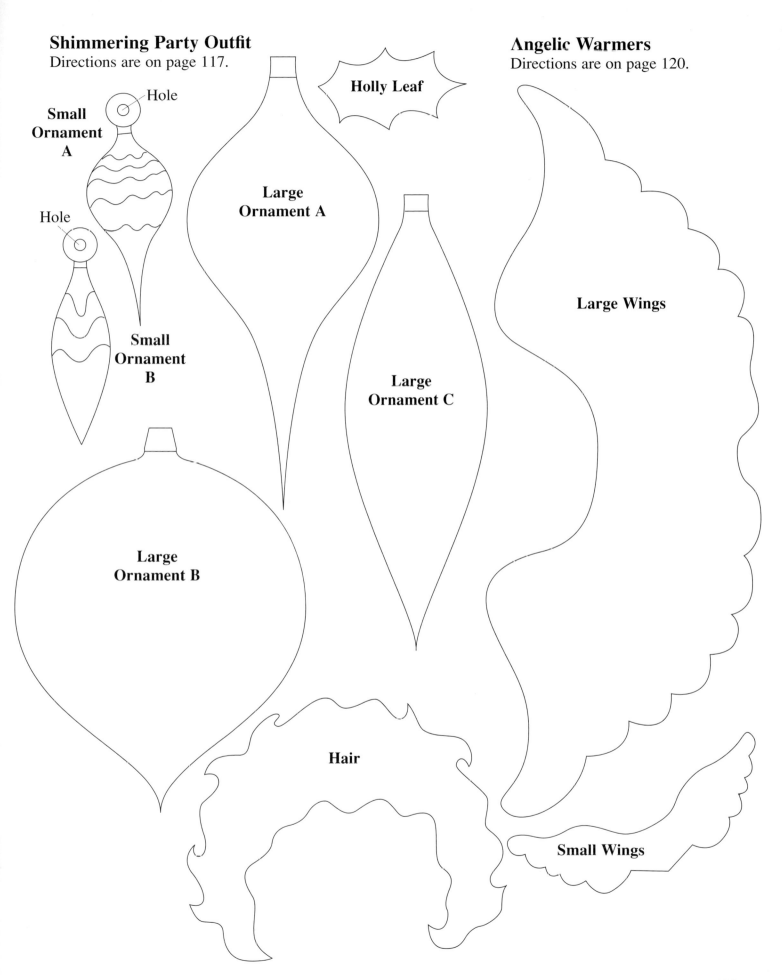

Shimmering Party Outfit
Directions are on page 117.

Small Ornament A

Hole

Hole

Small Ornament B

Large Ornament A

Holly Leaf

Large Ornament C

Large Ornament B

Hair

Angelic Warmers
Directions are on page 120.

Large Wings

Small Wings

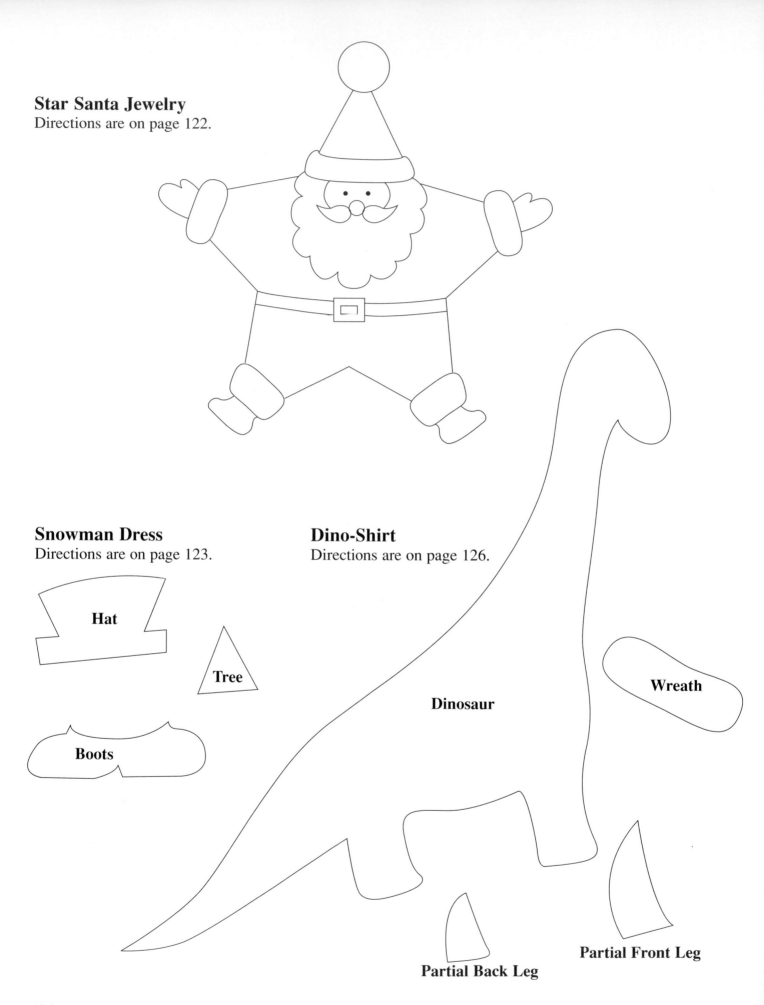

Star Santa Jewelry
Directions are on page 122.

Snowman Dress
Directions are on page 123.

Hat

Tree

Boots

Dino-Shirt
Directions are on page 126.

Dinosaur

Wreath

Partial Back Leg

Partial Front Leg

Sponge-Painted Bibs
Directions are on page 127.

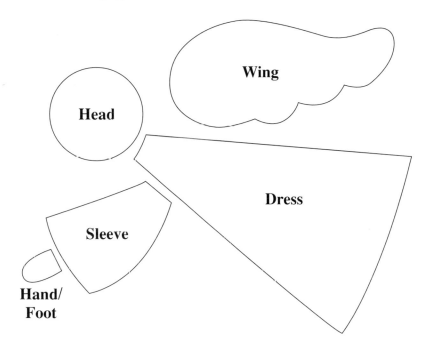

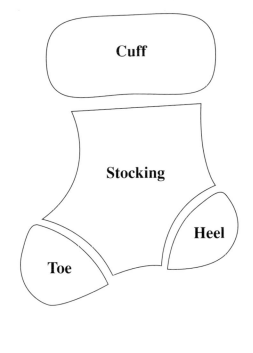

Wearables Kids Can Make:
Reindeer Sleep Shirt
Directions are on page 129.

Wearables Kids Can Make:
Decorated Shoes
Directions are on page 128.

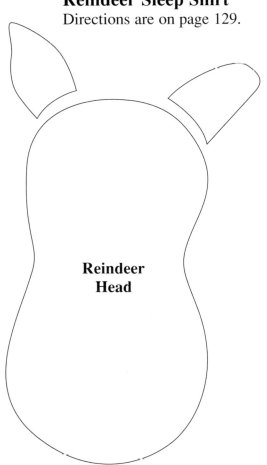

Tips for Better Crafting

In the following pages, Heidi shares her secrets to crafting success. Learn how to stock your supply room, which glue to use, and much, much more.

General Supplies

Here are some of the supplies you'll need to make many of the craft projects in this book.
- Waxed paper, paper towels, toothpicks
- Florist's pins and straight pins
- Several 3" squares of lightweight cardboard for squeegees
- White paper, tracing paper, or Shrink-It Plastic for transferring patterns
- Ruler or measuring tape
- Pencils and colored pencils
- Paintbrushes (½" flat shader, fine-tip, and sponge brushes)
- Pieces of pop-up craft sponge
- Fine-tip permanent black marker
- Rubber bands and clothespins to hold things together while glue is drying
- Scissors (separate scissors for fabric, all-purpose scissors for use with paper and other craft materials, heavy-duty scissors or wire cutters for use with florist's wire and other hard-to-cut items, as well as decorative blade scissors)

To keep from applying too much glue, cut a 3" square of cardboard and use it as a squeegee to smooth a film of glue onto your craft material.

Choosing Your Glue

Heidi relied upon the extensive line of Aleene's products to make the projects in this book. To help you determine which glue is best suited for your general crafting, refer to the handy list below.
- **Aleene's Tacky Glue™** is an excellent all-purpose glue for crafting. It is especially suited for working with fabric but is not for use with wearables because it is not washable.
- **Aleene's Designer Tacky Glue™** is a thicker, tackier version of Tacky Glue and is intended for use with hard-to-hold items like Fun Foam.
- **Aleene's Jewel-It™ and OK to Wash-It™** glues are designed for use with wearables and other fabric items that will need to be washed. In particular, use Jewel-It to adhere acrylic jewels or decorative buttons to wearables or home decor items.

The glues are nontoxic and ACMI (Art and Craft Materials Institute) approved. The glues dry clear and flexible, making them excellent for crafting.

Hints for Successful Gluing

To make Tacky Glue or Designer Tacky Glue even tackier, leave the lid off for about an hour before use so that excess moisture evaporates.

Too much glue makes items slip around; it does not provide a better bond. To apply a film of glue to fabric or brown bag, use a cardboard squeegee. Simply cut a 3" square of cardboard (cereal box cardboard works well) and use this squeegee to smooth the glue onto the craft material. Wait a few minutes to let the glue begin to form a skin before putting the items together.

To use Jewel-It to attach a jewel or a button to a project, squeeze a puddle of glue on the project where you want your jewel to be placed. Press the jewel into the glue puddle so that the glue comes up around the sides of the jewel.

Transferring Patterns

Before you begin any project, read the directions all the way through and look at the patterns for additional important information. Then gather all the necessary materials and supplies as listed in the materials list or the directions to begin work on your chosen design.

Your first step in making a craft project usually involves transferring a pattern from the book to your craft material. To transfer a pattern, lay a piece of tracing paper or lightweight white paper (for a longer-lasting pattern, use Aleene's Opake Shrink-It™ Plastic instead) on top of the printed pattern. Trace the pattern, using a pencil or a marker. Be sure to transfer any details, like placement markings and facial features, to the tracing paper. Cut out the pattern.

When only half a pattern is given, fold the tracing paper in half and place the fold on the broken line of the pattern. Trace the pattern as printed and cut out through both layers. Unfold the paper for the complete pattern.

To transfer the pattern to the craft material, lay the pattern on the material as specified in the directions. Trace, using a pencil or a pen for paper, wood, or cardboard and a disappearing-ink fabric marker for fabrics.

To reverse a pattern when your craft material has a right and wrong side, trace the pattern onto paper and cut it out as described above. To transfer to fusible web or a print fabric, lay the pattern right side down on the paper side of the web or the wrong side of the fabric; trace and cut out.

To reverse a pattern to make a matched set of pieces, trace the pattern piece onto the craft material once and then flip the pattern over and trace again. When your craft material has no right or wrong side, it is not necessary to reverse the pattern for matched pieces.

Metric Conversion Chart

U.S.	Metric
⅛"	3 mm
¼"	6 mm
⅜"	9 mm
½"	1.3 cm
⅝"	1.6 cm
¾"	1.9 cm
⅞"	2.2 cm
1"	2.5 cm
2"	5.1 cm
3"	7.6 cm
4"	10.2 cm
5"	12.7 cm
6"	15.2 cm
7"	17.8 cm
8"	20.3 cm
9"	22.9 cm
10"	25.4 cm
11"	27.9 cm
12"	30.5 cm
36"	91.5 cm
45"	114.3 cm
60"	152.4 cm
⅛ yard	0.11 m
¼ yard	0.23 m
⅓ yard	0.3 m
⅜ yard	0.34 m
½ yard	0.46 m
⅝ yard	0.57 m
⅔ yard	0.61 m
¾ yard	0.69 m
⅞ yard	0.8 m
1 yard	0.91 m

To Convert to Metric Measurements:

When you know:	Multiply by:	To find:
inches (")	25	millimeters (mm)
inches (")	2.5	centimeters (cm)
inches (")	0.025	meters (m)
feet (')	30	centimeters (cm)
feet(')	0.3	meters (m)
yards	90	centimeters (cm)
yards	0.9	meters (m)

Working with Aleene's Fusible Web

Aleene's Fusible Web™ makes no-sew projects faster and easier. For the best results, always wash and dry fabrics and garments to remove any sizing before applying fusible web. Do not use fabric softener in the washer or the dryer.

Lay the fabric wrong side up on the ironing surface. A hard surface, like a wooden cutting board, will ensure a firmer bond. Lay the fusible web, paper side up, on the fabric (the glue side feels rough). With a hot, dry iron, fuse the web to the fabric by placing and lifting the iron. Do not allow the iron to rest on the web for more than 1 or 2 seconds. Do not slide the iron back and forth across the web. Remember, you are only transferring the glue web to the fabric not completely melting the glue.

Transfer the pattern to the paper side of the web and cut out the pattern as specified in the project directions. Or referring to the right side of the fabric, cut out the desired portion from a print fabric.

To fuse the appliqué to the project, carefully peel the paper backing from the appliqué, making sure the web is attached to the fabric. If the web is still attached to the paper, re-fuse it to the appliqué before fusing the appliqué to the project. Arrange the appliqué on the prewashed fabric or other surface, as listed in the project directions. If you are fusing more that 1 appliqué, place all the appliqués in the desired position before fusing.

With a hot, dry iron, fuse the appliqués to the project by placing and lifting the iron. Hold the iron on each area of the appliqués for approximately 5 seconds. Applying lines of dimensional paint to the edges of your fused appliqués provides a finished look, but it is not necessary.

Handcrafted Means Hand-Wash

After you have created a beautiful wearable, you want to care for it properly. Be sure to let the glue or the paint on your new garment dry for at least 1 week before washing. This allows the embellishment to form a strong bond with the fabric. (For glitter designs, wait 2 weeks before washing.)

Turn the garment wrong side out, hand-wash, and hang to dry. Hand washing protects your hard work from the rough-and-tumble treatment of a washing machine.

Bread Dough Poinsettia How-to

To create the porcelain-like poinsettias used in the jewelry on page 108, you'll need to whip up a batch of bread dough. For 1 batch of red bread dough, you will need 1 slice of white bread with the crust removed, a plastic cup, 1 tablespoon of Aleene's Tacky Glue™, a wooden craft stick, and red acrylic paint.

Tear the bread into small pieces and put the pieces into a plastic cup. Add 1 tablespoon of glue to the bread and mix with the craft stick until a coarse ball forms. (*Hint:* If you coat your tablespoon with cold cream, the glue will come off more easily.) Remove the ball of dough from the cup.

With clean hands, knead the dough for about 5 minutes or until it is smooth and pliable. (*Note:* Be sure to wash your hands because any dirt on your hands will be transferred to the dough. If desired, rub your hands with cold cream to make the dough easier to work.) If the dough is too coarse, add a little more glue. The dough will stick to your hands until it becomes smooth.

To color the dough, flatten the dough ball in your hand, making a small well in the center of the dough. Pour a small amount of paint in the well. Knead the dough until the paint is incorporated.

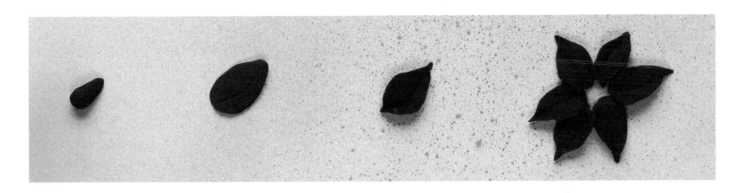

1 To make each large poinsettia petal, pinch off a pea-sized ball of dough. Roll and form the ball into a teardrop shape. Squeeze the teardrop between your fingers to flatten it into a petal. Use a straight pin to make an indentation in the top of the petal for the vein. Pinch each end of the petal to shape it. Let it dry. Repeat to make the number of large petals specified in the project directions. Arrange the petals in a circle, overlapping them as needed to get the desired effect.

2 To make each small poinsettia petal, pinch off a smaller than pea-sized ball of dough. Shape the dough as described in Step 1. Let it dry. Repeat to make the number of small petals specified in the project directions. Arrange the small petals on top of the large petals. Use Tacky Glue to glue all the petals together where they touch. Let the poinsettia dry.

Burnt Brown Bag How-to

Many years ago during a flammability test of Tacky Glue, the product testers discovered that burning a layer of wet glue resulted in a surface resembling metal sculpture. With these step-by-step directions, you'll learn how to do this simple technique.

To make burnt brown bag projects, you will need to gather the supplies mentioned in the materials list for the specific project. You will also need Aleene's Tacky Glue™, a candle, matches, and a scrap of fabric.

2 Using a scrap of fabric, gently wipe off the soot. If any brown bag shows through, the glue is not completely burned; hold the design over the flame again to finish the burning process. To create a textured surface, use the fabric scrap to mold the soft glue, slightly ruffling the surface. Let the design dry overnight.

1 Glue together layers of brown bag and cut out the pattern as specified in the project directions. Spread a fairly thick coat of glue on 1 side of the brown bag shape.

While the glue is still wet, hold the design, glue side down, directly over a candle flame. Hold the design as close to the flame as possible but don't snuff out the candle. Move the design around over the flame until all of the glue is black and sooty. (*Note:* The burning process takes 1½ to 2 minutes and will produce a little smoke.)

3 To add gold metallic highlights to a burnt brown bag design, squeeze a puddle of gold paste paint on a piece of waxed paper. Dip your finger into the paint and wipe off the excess paint on a paper towel. Gently rub your finger over the burnt design. Continue adding gold to the design until you get the desired effect. Let the design dry.

Shrink-It How-to

Make jewelry, refrigerator magnets, and many other kinds of projects with Aleene's Shrink-It™ Plastic. Children especially enjoy watching the designs shrink during baking. Keep the following tips in mind when working with Shrink-It.

Before using colored pencils on Shrink-It, thoroughly sand the Shrink-It with fine-grade sandpaper. Hold the Shrink-It up to a light source to check for unsanded areas.

Cut out your design and punch holes as specified in the project directions before shrinking, because it will be too hard to cut after shrinking. Wear a pair of cotton gloves to protect your hands while handling hot Shrink-It.

2 The edges of the design should begin to curl within 25 seconds; if not increase the temperature slightly. If the edges begin to curl as soon as the design is put in the oven, reduce the temperature. The design will curl and roll while it is shrinking. A large design may curl over onto itself. If this happens, open the oven and unfold the design; then continue baking.

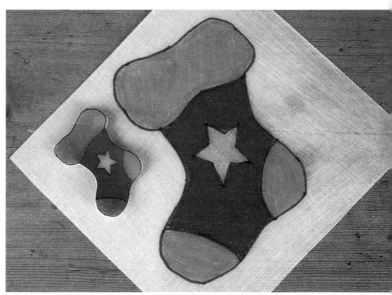

1 Preheat a toaster oven or a conventional oven to 275° to 300°. Sprinkle a room-temperature baking board or nonstick cookie sheet with baby powder to prevent sticking and to ensure even shrinking. Place the Shrink-It design on the prepared surface and put it in the oven.

3 After about 1 minute, the design will lie flat. Use a hot pad to remove the baking board from the oven. Use a spatula to move the design from the baking board to a flat surface. To keep the design flat during cooling, place a book on top of it. You may shape the design before it cools. If you are not happy with the shape of your design after it has cooled, return it to the oven for a few seconds to warm it again. Remove the design from the oven and reshape it while it is still hot. Then set it aside to cool completely.

141

Making a Multilooped Bow

For large bows, use either a stiff or wire-edged ribbon rather than a ribbon from a limp fabric like satin. For small bows, you may use satin ribbon. For a bow with a flat center, you will need to omit the first 3" loop. This will provide a space to glue on ribbon roses or charms as specified in the project directions.

If the ribbon does not have a distinguishable right side, choose which side will be the right side and twist the ribbon as directed below. Twisting the ribbon and grasping it firmly while making the bow ensures a fluffy bow.

Always take the ribbon width into consideration when determining the required yardage for a bow. With a wider ribbon, you won't need as many yards of ribbon.

Suggested yardages

- For a 5"-diameter bow, you will need about 2¾ yards of ½"- to 1"-wide ribbon.
- For a 7"-diameter bow, you will need about 3½ yards of 1"- to 1½"-wide ribbon.
- For a 9"-diameter bow, you will need about 4½ yards of 1½"- to 3"-wide ribbon.

2 Fold the long end of the ribbon under, forming a loop 1" to 2" long above the center loop. Gather the width of the ribbon and grasp it between your finger and thumb beneath the center loop. Hold the gathered areas of the ribbon firmly to ensure a tight bow. Twist the long end of the ribbon so that the right side is facing you.

1 With the right side of the ribbon facing you, leave a tail about 5" long and gather the width of the ribbon between the forefinger and the thumb of 1 hand. Twist the long end of the ribbon over so that the wrong side is facing you. Bring the long end of the ribbon toward you, forming a 3" loop on top of your thumb. Gather the width of the ribbon and grasp it between your finger and thumb. Twist the long end of the ribbon so that the right side is facing you. (*Note:* Omit the 3" loop at the center of the bow for a small bow for a craft project.)

3 Fold the long end of the ribbon under, forming a loop 1" to 2" long below the center loop. Gather the width of the ribbon and grasp it between your finger and thumb beneath the center loop. Twist the long end of the ribbon so that the right side is facing you.

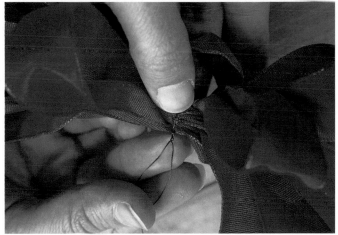

4 Repeat steps 2 and 3, forming 4 to 6 more loops about 1" to 2" long.

6 When the bow is the desired size, slip a 6" length of 18-gauge florist's wire through the center loop. Bend the wire at the center and twist it tightly around the twisted part of the bow to secure all the loops. Tightly twisted wire is the secret to a successful bow. Arrange the loops and the streamers as desired for a full bow.

5 Repeat steps 2 and 3, forming additional loops about 3" to 4" long until all the ribbon is used. Be sure to leave a tail about 5" long after the last loop. Always make loops in pairs, with 1 above the center of the bow and 1 below the center of the bow. As you add loops to the bow, don't build the loops right on top of each other. Pull some loops away from the center and toward the sides.

7 Trim the ribbon ends even, notching them or cutting them at an angle. To add additional streamers, cut a ribbon length that measures twice the desired streamer length. Gather the ribbon length at the center. With the right side of the ribbon facing the back of the bow, attach the ribbon to the bow, using the ends of the wire. Use the wire ends to attach the bow to another item. If the wire ends are not needed to attach the bow, trim the excess wire.

Index